# CHILD PROTECTION AND EARLY YEARS TEACHERS

## COPING WITH CHILD ABUSE

**Tricia David**

OPEN UNIVERSITY PRESS
Buckingham · Philadelphia

Open University Press
Celtic Court
22 Ballmoor
Buckingham
MK18 1XW

and

1900 Frost Road, Suite 101
Bristol, PA 19007, USA

First Published 1993

A catalogue record of this book is available
from the British Library

*Library of Congress Cataloging-in-Publication Data*

David, Tricia, 1942–
Child protection and early years teachers : coping with child
abuse / Tricia David
p.    cm.
Includes bibliographical references and index.
ISBN 0-335-09899-1. – ISBN 0-335-09894-0 (pbk.)
1. Abused children – Services for – Great Britain.  2. Child abuse –
Great Britain.  3. Early childhood teachers – Great Britain.
I. Title.
HV751.A6D38  1992
362.7′68′0941 – dc20                    92-16386
                                         CIP

Typeset by Colset Pte Ltd, Singapore
Printed in Great Britain by
J.W. Arrowsmith Ltd, Bristol

*In loving memory of
Joan and Frank Cullen*

# CONTENTS

# ACKNOWLEDGEMENTS

This book is the outcome of many of the different relationships and experiences I have had. Some have taken place during my years as a teacher and headteacher, and as a tutor on courses for teachers at initial and inservice levels, for parents, and for playgroup supervisors. Others, such as the relationships with my own parents and children, in which I consider myself to have been very fortunate, have also shaped my thinking about the way in which we treat young children in our society. I therefore have many, many people to thank, and I hope they will recognize the part they have all played in my evolving education. In particular I would like to acknowledge with gratitude: the comments on the manuscript made by my colleagues Ann Lewis and Frances Gardner (though any errors, misinterpretations or omissions remain my own responsibility); the contributions of staff at Open University Press; the Trustees of the Kellmer Pringle Foundation, who awarded me a Fellowship and funding for a multi-professional seminar series; the ideas and challenges provided by members of the Kellmer Pringle Seminar Series held at Warwick University in 1991–92; Roy, Sacha and Ceris, for 'being there'.

Although the title of my book seems to suggest that the best we can do is 'protect and cope', I hope early years teachers and educators will join me in advocating prevention, through the development of a society in which young children are valued and respected.

# ▪ PART ONE ▪

# UNDERSTANDING CHILD ABUSE

■ ONE ■

# CHILDREN: PEOPLE OR CHATTELS?

On 20 November 1989, the United Nations General Assembly adopted the UN Convention on Children's Rights. Although the most important aspect of the Convention may be the fact that at last children are to be recognized as human beings with rights – not chattels, objects for parents to dispose of as they will – for the focus of this book, Article 19 is central. This reads as follows:

1 States Parties shall take all appropriate legislative, administrative, social and educational measures to protect the child from all forms of physical or mental violence, injury or abuse, neglect or negligent treatment, maltreatment or exploitation including sexual abuse, while in the care of parent(s), legal guardian(s), or any other person who has the care of the child.

2 Such protective measures should, as appropriate, include effective procedures for the establishment of social programmes to provide necessary support for the child and for those who have the care of the child, as well as for other forms of prevention and for identification, reporting, referral, investigation, treatment and follow-up of instances of child maltreatment described heretofore, and as appropriate, for judicial involvement.

Department of Health (DoH) statistics for the end of March 1990 indicate that around four children in every 1000 aged under 18 in

the UK were on Child Protection Registers. Furthermore, according to the NSPCC (1989), the number of cases of child abuse registered by them doubled during the mid-1980s, from 1115 in 1985
to 2307 in 1987. Those who work in the field know that this may
represent only the tip of the iceberg, i.e. those cases where concern
had become so great and the evidence so certain that the children
in question were registered. The free national helpline for children
in distress, Childline, launched in October 1986, counselled over
47,000 children during its first two years. Its counsellors hear
children's anxieties and experiences of sexual and physical abuse,
as well as those relating to parental problems, such as divorce.
More recently, Childline has reported concern over the number of
children reporting being bullied in school. Many of the children who
ring the helpline state that they have not informed anyone else of
their problems.

If children feel that no-one close to them can be of help, that they
need to resort to phoning someone they do not know on a helpline,
what kind of a society do we live in? We must begin to ask many
questions about the causes and effects of abuse, and about ways of
*preventing* further violations, rather than operating from a purely
protectionist position. In the meantime, we must ask who the key
workers might be, and how they should operate.

In recent years, social services departments have been cut back,
despite the fact that a greater number of child abuse cases has
meant a heavier workload for social workers. After a period of
living abroad, one former social worker told me recently that she
does not intend returning to social services in the UK because the
vast majority of casework involves the investigation of child sexual
abuse, and the work is so poorly funded and staffed that rescue,
rather than prevention, is the order of the day.

The Children Act 1989, which came into force on 14 October
1991, revised the legislative framework for the emergency protection of children. The Act includes changes in procedure which
are intended to make it easier to secure the conviction of abusers,
by enabling children's evidence to be heard in court without the
kind of trauma experienced by them under earlier arrangements.
Further, this does away with the unfounded notion that children are
incapable of giving accurate evidence (Spencer and Flin 1990). In
future, video-recordings of interviews with children suspected
of being abused will be allowed as evidence, so long as there
is a television link to the courtroom, which can be used for later

cross-examination of the child. In this way, children will not have to come face to face with those they are accusing of the abuse, and one hopes that our adversarial legal system will be tempered in the case of child witnesses, such that children will be protected from the intimidating methods of defence lawyers.

One of the main, underpinning principles of the Children Act 1989 is the requirement for workers from statutory and voluntary agencies to work together effectively in support of families. The Cleveland child abuse inquiry (Butler-Sloss 1988) brought into sharp focus a fact that has been reiterated time after time in other child abuse inquiry reports – that professionals had not always, despite their intent, made the child's interests paramount, and further, that they had failed to work together effectively.

During my years as a teacher and headteacher in nursery and primary schools, I was aware that child protection work was an essential part of my role, because what was happening to children outside the school affected their ability to learn and to enjoy the opportunities offered them. I was aware that parents who abuse their children physically, emotionally and through neglect, are often themselves victims of a system which does not seem to care about them and which causes their lives to be one long struggle; many of them had themselves been victims of abuse. I was not alone at the time in thinking that sexual abuse was a very rare occurrence, committed by monsters. Because of this assumption, I was simply blind to the possibility that any of the children I taught could have been experiencing such unacceptable treatment at the hands of those who claimed to love them. Yet it is possible, statistically, that I was failing three children in every class of 30 I taught.

What I learned about child protection, my own role and that of other workers, was purely incidental, self-taught and with the assistance of the headteachers I worked with. Others have not been so lucky. Some, even now, work in schools where child abuse is assumed to be someone else's problem, or it is not seen as possible in the school's catchment area. All of us wish that the abuse of children was a thing of the past in our so-called civilized society. Sadly, there is mounting evidence that child abuse is occurring in all strata of society, and that abusers are increasingly found to be older children (see, e.g. Bentovim *et al.* 1991), making the issue of teacher involvement in prevention work not just unavoidable but vital.

Although the term 'fortunate' is not really appropriate in this context, I was in a sense fortunate in that I worked in an area in which health, social services and education personnel, together with probation service staff, developed collaborative styles of working in support of families. Hopefully, the guidelines laid down by the new edition of *Working Together* (DoH 1991c) and the intentions of the Children Act 1989 will mean that *everyone* involved in the protection of children will regard the child's interests as paramount; will work effectively with representatives of other agencies; will understand their own role, and that of others; will ensure full parental understanding of the unfolding events; and will be able to contribute fully to the process.

Nursery and infant teachers and other early childhood educators are at the heart of this process, because they are in almost daily contact with our youngest children. It is unlikely that children in this age range will be those using Childline, yet we know from the statistics that they too are represented among children subject to all forms of abuse (see NSPCC 1989). What this means is that teachers and other educators have a particular responsibility to ensure that small children know that they have someone to whom they can report their suffering: they need a friend. In early childhood provision, we pride ourselves that we regard the care and education of young children as inseparable, that we care for and care about the children who come into contact with us. This book is an attempt to offer some background knowledge, some analysis of research, some ideas about explanations for child abuse. It also offers for consideration some views on the ways in which schools can develop more effective child protection practice, both the *reactive* work involving cases of suspected abuse and the *proactive* work which is intended to eradicate suffering for the present and for future generations. The task will not be an easy one, and there are many questions for which we have no answers – or at best many 'maybes'. The only way we can begin to work towards some answers is by thinking, training and working together, and by sharing ideas about effective practice. To become friends to little children, we must also become friends to ourselves, to our colleagues and to parents. Further, we must become advocates of the changes needed in society which schools alone cannot achieve.

# TWO

# A TWENTIETH-CENTURY CHILDHOOD

In Chapter 1, I pointed out the staggering increase in the number of children registered as 'at risk' during the mid-1980s. Does this mean that the incidence of child abuse has increased during the last few years and that we are becoming more violent towards children than ever before? The most likely explanation is that we have become more aware, and that rates of detection have increased as levels of awareness have increased. Why should this be so?

First, our attitudes to the way in which the most vulnerable members of our society – women, children and animals – should be treated have changed. Aries (1962), De Mause (1974), Donzelot (1980) and Sommerville (1982) document the changes in societal perceptions of children and childhood in the West. Postman (1985) relates how children, after babyhood, used to be seen as miniature adults and dressed as such, entering into every aspect of life, from war and work to sexual activity and attendance at deathbeds. Breughel's paintings offer us a glimpse into this world with its lack of differentiation between children and adults. Postman suggests that it was the advent of the printing press which began the movement towards perceiving children as 'unfinished'. Suddenly, in order to be regarded as an adult and to be respected, one had to learn those skills defined as 'adult skills', and these have taken an increasingly longer period to acquire. Reflecting again on Breughel's representations, we can see that around the same time as literacy became necessary, it became inappropriate for adults to play children's games, adult leisure being channelled into certain accepted pursuits, such as fox-hunting, fishing, dancing, needle-work and so on.

Furthermore, attitudes towards children and childhood were subject to basic religious philosophies. The Catholic Church acted on the belief that children's innocence and purity could save human-kind. In one important example of this, Savonarola, a Florentine friar, involved in the Church's fifteenth-century movement to rescue boys from the clutches of a depraved society by providing schools, encouraged children to inform on their parents. Once information pertaining to the possession of books on magic, beauty aids, dice and indecent paintings had been passed on, Savonarola's followers would organize police raids, and the possessions – 'the vanities' – were taken away to be destroyed in great bonfires. Aries (1962) has suggested that interest in children and childhood increased as Chris-tianity gained greater influence.

Sommerville (1982) argues that the highest point reached by 'childhood' in Western culture was at the beginning of the twentieth century. During the nineteenth century, the aristocratic British, having visited America, returned declaring that there were no children there, since the outspoken and knowing young of America appeared very different from their own, innocent offspring. That children in the Jago (a London ghetto), or other poor areas of the country where the young were forced early in life to become respon-sible for their own and other family members' survival, might also be more precocious than their own children, never occurred to them. Nor did these facts cause them to recognize that they were laying on their own children a special role: 'to symbolize the inno-cence which a severely repressed society felt it had lost' (Sommerville 1982: 177).

While the children of rich and middle-class families were kept insulated, sanitized and in good health (relative to earlier times and poorer groups), the living conditions of working-class families had deteriorated. Rural families were usually poor and struggling to make ends meet, and in Ireland in particular people were leaving the land rather than starve to death. As the factories of the Indus-trial Revolution mushroomed, so agricultural workers descended upon the towns in which they were located.

By the mid-nineteenth century, the infant mortality rate stood at 2 per cent; it had earlier stood at over 50 per cent in certain parts of Britain, as people flocked to cities like Manchester. Many families – often large in size due to the lack of birth control – lived in abject poverty in crowded and unhygienic homes, like the cellars described by contemporary writers such as Mrs Gaskell. Young children frequently died of diseases caused by poor sanitation and an inadequate diet, and there was a lack of funds for medical attention. The history of working-class people in Britain is depicted as often cruel, demanding and dangerous (see, for example, the writings of E.P. Thompson, Flora Thompson, George Orwell and Margaret McMillan, or Carolyn Steedman (1990) on Margaret McMillan's publications about young children at the turn of the century).

Young children had to work long hours at unguarded machinery, and were beaten if they fell asleep or 'shirked'. We are often horrified by television documentaries showing children in developing countries who have been maimed in an effort to make their lives as beggars more lucrative, or working long hours manufacturing carpets. Yet about 100 years ago, it was usual to find the same in the countries now comprising the (so-called) First World. It may be that some of the practices we accept now as perfectly legitimate and 'normal' ways to treat children will seem cruel and exploitative when viewed retrospectively 100 years hence.

Our expectations of the standards of living appropriate for the upbringing of children have risen, as has our awareness of the rights of every citizen, rich or poor. Yet we are still experiencing the remnants of an era when 'spare the rod and spoil the child' was held as a firm belief. EPOCH, the campaign to end the smacking of children by parents, is not without its opponents, just as STOPP, the parallel schools' campaign, also met opposition. In some families, one is still aware of the strength of the ideas embodied in 'children should be seen and not heard' and 'an Englishman's home is his castle'. All of these beliefs rest on the assumption that parents, especially the father as head of the household – 'the master' (still a phrase used in everyday conversation in the Potteries, for example) – can treat children as their property. This ideology has been so strong and all-pervasive, that many people are unable to recognize it as one constructed to suit a particular group of people, to maintain their position of power, or a particular social system.

The lives of contemporary 'street children' in Brazil may not be far removed from the lives of many Victorian poor. Child prostitution was rife in London, for example, and the names of Lord

Shaftesbury and Dr Barnado are two we link historically with campaigns aimed at raising social awareness of the plight of working, homeless and poor children.

When one considers the difficulties working-class men – and then women – had in gaining the vote and in gaining rights as human beings and citizens, it is hardly surprising that children's rights have been neglected. In fact, child abuse was first brought to the headlines in 1874 under the auspices of an animal protection campaign in New York. A young girl named Mary Ellen, who lived with her adoptive parents, was regularly beaten and neglected by them. Her neighbours became concerned, though the adoptive parents saw no fault in their actions, as they 'owned' the child. The case was eventually brought to the attention of Henry Bergh, the founder of the Society for the Prevention of Cruelty to Animals, who brought a court action against the parents. Although there were more laws relating to the protection of animals than children at the time, the case was won on the basis of Mary's *human* rights, not – as is sometimes thought – because Mary Ellen was a member of an animal species. The lawyer who was hired by Henry Bergh subsequently precipitated the development of a new movement, the Society for the Prevention of Cruelty to Children, in December 1874.

The idea that children were not simply the property of the adults with whom they lived crossed the Atlantic. Perhaps as a result of the climate of opinion – then in flux because the women's rights movement had gained momentum – the National Society for the Prevention of Cruelty to children (NSPCC) was formed in the UK, and in 1889 the Prevention of Cruelty Act was passed. For the first time in British history, magistrates were empowered to issue warrants for private homes to be entered and children to be removed if maltreatment could be proven.

However, there was – and probably still is – a dilemma as regards the standards expected of families. Abuse, at first only recognized in the forms of physical abuse and neglect, needed to be severe before it was drawn to the attention of the authorities or a prosecution brought, since it was generally accepted in society that parents needed to chastise their children. Many of my own generation were brought up thinking we were lucky to have parents who did not hit us as a matter of course, and the research carried out by John and Elizabeth Newson (1963, 1968) probably created little of a stir even in the 1960s, when it was revealed that the majority of parents smacked their one-year-olds and that only 3 per cent of all four-year-olds were reportedly never smacked: three-quarters of four-year-olds were said to be smacked at least once a week. However, other parents were shocked at the suggestion that they might hit their tiny children. So, in the 1960s, as today, there were two very polarized camps in the UK – one believing it acceptable to strike children 'for their own good', the other seeing corporal punishment as a form of cruelty.

The advocates of smacking might argue that this permissiveness became endemic in the 1960s, leading to indiscipline. The counter-argument comes from Sweden, where corporal punishment was made illegal in 1979, despite a counter-lobby claiming state interference in a family's right to bring children up according to religious or other beliefs. In fact, measuring state interference in family life by comparing the numbers of children in compulsory care in Sweden (2.7 per 1000) and the UK (3.5 per 1000) in 1986, may be an indication that laying down clear guidelines about such matters as physical abuse may not be considered interference after all. A large-scale survey conducted in 1981 and again in 1988 by Professor Adrienne Haeuser (reported in Newell 1989) concluded that while Swedish parents seemed to have become more conservative, traditional and restricting, in other words less permissive, over the seven-year period, they still accepted the limits set on physical punishment. Haeuser suggests that the example set for each generation, the adult role models of appropriate adult behaviour towards children, is transmitted from one generation to the next and the use of force is gradually eradicated.

During the same period in which the Newsons were conducting their research, a survey conducted for the Plowden Committee (CACE 1967) indicated that 88.3 per cent of teachers were in favour of corporal punishment 'as a last resort', and one can surmise that it was as a result of the committee members' visits to various schools that the report made a strong statement in favour of learning being conducted in schools without a 'sword of Damocles' hanging over the children's heads.

The Children's Legal Centre (Newell 1989) recently carried out a survey of the views of Members of Parliament and discovered that only 11 per cent of Conservative and 69 per cent of Labour MPs were against the use of corporal punishment by parents, and of these many would not commit themselves to the legal prohibition of such treatment, as in Sweden and Finland. In fact, in 1988, Edwina

Currie MP replied to a letter from the Children's Legal Centre to the effect that the government considered current legislation adequate, and that a law concerned with domestic corporal punishment would be unworkable. It may be that the most recent changes in attitudes towards the position of women in the home – for example, rulings on rape within marriage, police action on domestic violence – herald a growing climate of opinion about the misuse of power 'behind closed doors'.

In schools, at least, it would appear that perceptions of how adults should behave towards children have changed more rapidly over the last five years than they did in the previous 100 years, for it was only in 1987 (more than a century after the French) that corporal punishment became illegal in maintained schools in the UK (it is still permissible in private schools). In fact, the UK was the only European Community country still to retain corporal punishment in its schools in 1983. Somehow, we have a society which has clung on to the idea that hitting people will make them good, clever, hardworking and, one suspects, obedient.

What I am arguing here is that we should examine our expectations, the rules and who makes them, etc., for I have found that children are generally very fair, and when involved in decision making about rules of conduct, only need an occasional reminder. To reiterate the title of Peter Newell's (1989) book, which argues the case against smacking, *Children are People Too*. It is often when children are becoming ill, when they do not understand and are confused or afraid, or feel unloved, that they 'do wrong'. In other words, when people punish children, it is often as a result of fault on the part of the punisher, or the constraints of the system in which the adult operates, that the children have erred:

> Must childhood and adolescence inevitably be periods of life when adults protect, prohibit and know best? To what extent is biology and to what extent are social factors responsible for the phenomenon of childhood? . . . there is the controversy over the roles played by poverty, class and race within our society, for it seems to be the children of the poor and of minority groups who receive the bulk of the attention from courts, police and social welfare agencies. (King 1981b: 2)

As Michael King suggests, we must examine the ways in which certain groups have been pathologized and marginalized. It is actually quite difficult at times to differentiate what is truly a cruel way in which to treat children, so that the parents involved need to be given help to remediate the situation, or have others take over from them, and what, for example, white middle-class workers interpret as poor treatment because they do not understand a different, but legitimate, subculture. A good way of illustrating this difference might be a reversal, the fact that most working-class parents find it difficult to understand how the rich can possibly claim to love their children, yet send them away to boarding school at an early age. What may appear to many members of the population as a form of emotional (and possibly also physical) child abuse, is obviously meant to be 'the making of them', the way in which cultural capital, the power through certain forms of knowledge, vested in that class, is passed on within the subcultural group. Thus it is labelled positively and not categorized as a form of abuse by those defining accepted parenting in our society.

The figures for suspected abuse of all kinds are questionable. While the levels of abuse are reported to be higher in poor and working-class areas, this may be due to detection rates as a result of closer monitoring rather than to real incidences. Additionally, some believe that middle-class parents are more able to conceal events from neighbours and investigating workers. Certainly, one must remain sceptical across the whole spectrum of abuse. While stressful living conditions, such as an inadequate diet, poor housing, a lack of finance and a lack of nursery provision, may have a more marked effect on parents in poorer areas (and the higher representation of working-class mothers of young children at the outpatient clinics of mental hospitals bears this out; see Brown and Harris 1978), leading to a potential for non-accidental injury, nevertheless some forms of abuse, such as emotional and sexual abuse, are thought to occur across all groups, and even physical abuse may be more widespread than initially thought among the better off.

An international survey of university students (Berger *et al.* 1988) found that 80 per cent reported having been spanked in childhood. However, less than 3 per cent perceived themselves as having been physically abused, even though some had, in the course of being punished, received broken limbs, burns, cuts, bruises, head and dental injuries – perhaps a sad portent for their own future behaviour as parents.

Had these been very young children, the difficulty in accepting the inappropriateness of the treatment might have been understandable, depending as it does on the stage of moral development. I remember my daughters, aged four and six, returning home from a teatime visit to some of their friends and relating the following account. While playing in their friends' garden they had observed Daryl, a boy from the six-year-olds' class at school, in his family garden next door. Suddenly, Daryl's mother emerged from the house shouting at him for some misdemeanour and then she beat him with a stick. When I exclaimed in horror, my elder daughter, whom I had expected to feel shocked at such an episode, announced in a matter-of-fact tone, 'Well, he was very naughty.'

Kohlberg's (1969) work on the development of moral understanding becomes a central consideration in our discussions of how children should be treated by adults. Children themselves, while not liking the effects of severe punishment, may accept, in their view, an adult's right to perpetrate such acts on them by dint of the authority apparently vested in that adult. When young, they may never come to question the final, exasperated 'Because I say so' of a hard-pressed parent, or the right of a parent to slap them, if they recognize they were in the wrong.

That some adults never develop beyond this stage of moral development, particularly in relation to their own role as parents, may be the result of a number of factors. First, it could be that these parents are not very intelligent and are therefore unable to conceptualize other ways of being. Secondly, it might be due to a lack of opportunities to consider the kinds of behaviour appropriate for an adult to adopt with small children, or those weaker than themselves. Thirdly, it could be that their own life experiences have only offered them role models who were never to be questioned, always right and who maintained their authority with the stick and the carrot (extrinsic rewards), rather than fostering inner control, i.e. self-discipline based on reason, humanity and justice.

## The Children Act 1989

The concepts of reason, humanity and justice are enshrined in an important and unprecedented piece of legislation which is intended to alter radically the way children are treated in British society. The 1989 Children Act, which came into force in October 1991, is based on fundamental principles, two of which are contingent upon the nationwide development of newer thinking about children and childhood. The first of these is the idea of *parental responsibility*.

Earlier legislation has tended to enshrine parental rights. This new emphasis on parental responsibility and what 'a reasonable parent' might do will no doubt provide the meat for many a future courtroom debate, but, nevertheless, it presents society with a fresh way of looking at the parent–child relationship. Perhaps at last we will see an end to the 'ownership mentality' which may have led to many cases of maltreatment – 'I can do what I like with what is mine'. Responsibility, rather than rights, brings with it notions of parental duties and obligations to children, and where parents find difficulty in fulfilling these tenets of the new law, local authorities are charged with the responsibility of helping parents. We in Britain do seem to be confused about the extent to which the agencies of 'the state' should have power in relation to families. We have witnessed a period when social workers have been accused of being too interventionist *and* too reluctant to intervene. The tragedy is that it may be impossible for us to totally eradicate child abuse unless we change the way society is structured, yet social workers must bear the brunt of society's confusion.

The second principle which could have an effect on the way children are perceived in society is that of *the child's welfare as paramount*, and this includes a requirement that where courts are involved in decisions about children the child's voice must be heard. The old 'adults know best' attitude will actually be unlawful, and teachers may become actively involved as advocates, ensuring that children's views really are listened to, since they may be the adults who interact most closely with children on a daily basis and who will therefore be known and trusted by them. The other two fundamental principles on which the Act is based are the importance of having due regard for the child's 'racial origin, cultural and linguistic background', which those of us working in the field of education have been sensitive to for some time now, with varying degrees of success, and the requirement for all agencies to work collaboratively, which I will consider more fully in Chapter 14.

Therefore, 1989 proved an important year as far as rhetoric regarding children was concerned, with the passing of the Children Act, the United Nations Convention on Children's Rights, and the effects of Britain's membership of the European Community (children within the other member states enjoy greater recognition as people in their own right). As I suggested earlier, the Children Act 1989 is a step away from the type of society which promulgates the view that children are the property of the adults they live with. The 'children as property' view fosters an inability to see children as individuals with feelings, and they then become objects on which to vent one's anger, insecurities or sexual aberrations.

In many ways, it seems incredible that we have failed to recognize the personhood of children, because each of us has been a child and should be able to remember, if not everything about our own childhood, at least some of the happiest and definitely the most traumatic events. In a sense, our own experiences have in fact indoctrinated us into seeing children as subordinate, less important than the adults  we have now grown up to be. We need to be alert to indications that our current construction of childhood is only slowly changing to accept that children themselves shape their own lives as much as they are *allowed.*

# THREE

# WHAT IS CHILD ABUSE AND NEGLECT?

Child abuse is difficult to define, because, as I will discuss later, what is defined as abuse is culturally determined. Four forms of abuse are currently recognized in the UK, about which statistics are kept by the NSPCC and the National Children's Homes (NCH). These are: *physical abuse, sexual abuse, emotional abuse* and *neglect*. In 1988, the then Department of Health and Social Security (DHSS) and the Welsh Office issued *Working Together* (1988; DoH 1991c), a booklet of guidelines intended to facilitate inter-agency cooperation. The booklet was produced after consultation with a wide range of agencies, including fieldworkers. That the categories for registration of cases of child abuse are not claimed to be exhaustive is an indication of the kind of open-minded attitude it is important we retain in decisions about what constitutes child abuse in a complex and evolving, pluralistic society. The guidelines stress the need for practitioners to be aware that different forms of abuse may be suffered simultaneously by a child – the categories are not mutually exclusive.

*Working Together* defines the forms of abuse as follows, prefacing the definitions with the statement that:

. . . harm may be the result of a direct act or by a failure to act to provide proper care, or both:

*Neglect:* The persistent or severe neglect of a child (for example, by exposure to any kind of danger, including starvation) which results in serious impairment of the child's health or development, including non-organic failure to thrive.

*Physical abuse*: Physical injury to a child, including deliberate poisoning, where there is definite knowledge, or a reasonable suspicion, that the injury was inflicted or knowingly not prevented.

*Sexual abuse*: The involvement of dependent, developmentally immature children and adolescents in sexual activities they do not truly comprehend, to which they are unable to give informed consent, or that violate the social taboos of family roles.

*Emotional abuse*: The severe adverse effect on the behaviour and emotional development of a child caused by persistent or severe emotional ill-treatment or rejection. All abuse involves some emotional ill-treatment; this category should be used where it is the main or sole form of abuse. (DHSS 1988: para. 5.31)

As a result of anxieties about children who do not fall neatly into any of the above main categories, a further definition was introduced, that of grave concern:

*Grave concern*: Children whose situations do not fit the above categories, but where social and medical assessments indicate that they are at significant risk of abuse. These could include situations where another child in the household has been harmed or the household contains a known abuser. (DHSS 1988: para. 5.31)

The 1991 version of *Working Together* has slightly modified these definitions, for example prefacing some with 'the actual or likely . . .', thus dispensing with the category of 'grave concern'. Additionally, perhaps as a result of difficulties with definitions, paragraph 6.41 states:

. . . The Courts may well provide an interpretation of 'sexual abuse' (which is not defined in the Act) which is different from that used in particular cases, in which case their definition should be used in relation to those cases. (DoH 1991c: para. 6.41; The Act referred to is the Children Act 1989)

The disagreements over definitions, categories and severity of harm or injuries suffered by children has caused abuse research to flounder – comparisons are impossible if different groups of researchers or practitioners or the public recognize different events, or degrees of harm, as constituting abuse. Similarly, practitioners are subject to identical dilemmas about whether a case should be reported and registered, especially where the abuse, say severe chastisement of a small child, is permissible, culturally accepted and determined, or illegal and a denial of the rights and personhood of that child. When there is obvious injury to a child, it is sometimes difficult to decide whether it is an isolated accident, or evidence of persistent, deliberate or neglectful harm. The worker has to try to ascertain whether evidence is present in the condition of the injured child, or any other child in the same household, that abuse has occurred. This highlights the reason why teachers in particular have a role to play in recording data about bruising, cigarette burns, and so on.

The NSPCC statistics for 1987 indicate that the cases of physical abuse reported involved the following types of injuries to children: serious head injuries, long bone fractures, soft tissue damage, attempted strangulation, drowning, suffocation, ingestion, convulsions and concussion (Gilmour 1988).

Martin was admitted to a nursery school on his third birthday, at the request of the local social services department. He was already registered as 'at risk' of physical abuse, following admission to hospital with what staff felt were non-accidental injuries. Martin lived with his mother, Susan, who had become pregnant during her only long-term relationship: the man was married and, on learning of the pregnancy, demanded that Susan have an abortion, or their relationship was at an end. Susan carried on with the pregnancy, she 'lost' her 'lover' and was subjected to severe disapproval from her parents, who had in fact, according to Susan herself, emotionally abused her as a child, always showing their preference for her prettier and more able sister.

Martin settled into life in the nursery school well. The staff were pleased at his keen interest in the available activities and his obvious happiness – he would often sing as he played and he would listen with rapt attention to stories, having a host of intelligent questions to ask.

The school had built up good relationships with local social services offices (several different 'patches' covered the nursery's 'catchment' area) and the social worker assigned to the case was pleased with Martin's progress, but still unsure of the effects of

Susan's violently fluctuating moods. All of the professionals involved worked from the basic assumption that they needed to support, encourage and empower Susan. The nursery staff and the social worker gave Susan as much attention and positive feedback as they could, in order to raise her self-esteem, but one group for whom she seemed to have only contempt was the nurses and doctors at the local hospital. Susan claimed that Martin had a severe hearing problem. She had taken Martin to the hospital and had been told there was nothing whatsoever wrong with his hearing. Undeterred, Susan made demands for further appointments at the hospital. On the day the appointment was due, Martin attended the nursery with obvious signs of bleeding from one ear. The headteacher asked him about this and Martin replied that his Mummy had 'had to clean his ears for the doctor'. The headteacher had never seen any signs of bleeding from Martin's ears before. It was impossible for her to judge whether the bleeding was the result of Susan's over-enthusiastic attention to presenting herself as a mother who took proper care of her child's cleanliness, or the result of inadvertently disturbing an infected ear, or deliberate probing of the ear with the intention of vindicating herself over her claim that Martin had an ear problem. The link with the social worker, and through her to the hospital staff, was vital, collaborative practice.

Under the 1989 Children Act, neglected children should be in a position to receive greater attention than they have to date. The ability to respond to all children 'in need' will lie with the levels of resourcing available to local authorities. In relation to children whose families may be unable or unwilling to fulfil their needs, or prevent them from harmful conditions, the Children Act defines 'a child in need' as being:

> . . . unlikely to achieve or maintain, or to have the opportunity of achieving or maintaining, a reasonable standard of health or development without the provision for him of services by a local authority . . . his health or development is likely to be significantly impaired, or further impaired, without the provision for him of such services. (Children Act 1989: part III)

The Children Act 1989 places a general duty on local authorities to safeguard and promote the welfare of children in need living in their area. Because the principles of the Act include the belief that children 'are generally best looked after within the family'

(DoH 1990: 1), local authorities are required to give families whatever support they need to prevent ill-treatment and neglect. Neglect and malnutrition can result in permanent damage to young children, since certain nutrients are needed for growth, brain functioning, learning and the development of intelligence. Neglect and emotional deprivation can be hidden causes of 'failure to thrive'. Nursery staff can monitor children's growth, recording their height and weight as part of ongoing learning activities. Parents can be involved in such activities as part of normal, everyday life in school, and thus any anxieties on the part of staff can be raised in the course of the events, rather than in any recriminatory fashion.

Whether as the result of a lack of resources, or because there may be disagreements among adults from the professions or voluntary agencies involved as to the seriousness of a problem, action may or may not be taken in cases of neglect. This could involve not only the grassroots professionals and people working for voluntary agencies, but also the local politicians who must make budget demands of their officers. The Health Visitors' Association (HVA) was particularly concerned with the findings of a survey the association carried out just before implementation of the Children Act 1989. The HVA issued a press release in September 1991, stating that there were fears that health visitors were defining children 'in need' in a very narrow sense, i.e. children with severe mental or physical handicaps. In other words, children with other needs were being overlooked in relation to this category.

Jonathan Bradshaw's (1990) study of child poverty and deprivation in the UK, one of eight studies of industrialized countries, commissioned by the UNICEF International Child Development Centre in Florence, paints a depressing picture of life for families struggling to clothe, feed and house their children. Bradshaw quotes a random survey of poor families living in public sector housing in Edinburgh, Glasgow and London, which concluded that a third of the homes contained damp and almost half mould growth, with the consequent ill-effects on children's health. Asking why children are living in such conditions, and why families are unable to clothe and feed their children appropriately, rather than simply putting the children on the at-risk register, labelling the families as feckless and inadequate, and giving the parents loans and cast-offs, can lead one to tricky political reflection of the kind likely to attract the label of activist.

A headteacher of a first school working in an area where many of the families were living in poverty, discussed with the Education Welfare Officer (EWO) for the area, the inadequate clothing, lack of hygiene and suspected inadequacy of both sleep and food, which was particularly acute in the case of one six-year-old boy. The head, believing that it should be the right of every child in the UK today to be warm, clean, fed and have a comfortable, dry, warm place to sleep, hoped the EWO might be able to act by defining the child as neglected. The EWO argued that almost every child on the estate was living in similar conditions. What the headteacher could not understand was the reduction in expectations. Had this child been the only one so deprived, living in an area where other children's quality of life compared more favourably, such as those on a neighbouring estate, would action have been more likely? This case predated the implementation of the 1989 Children Act, but the question it raises still remains. We will have to wait for future evaluations of the effects of the Act, and the arrangements made by local authorities for optimal use of the resources they possess, to assess the real effects the legislation has had on the lives of children.

The emotional needs of individual children may vary widely. Some young children appear to be very confident, sure of the love and esteem in which they are held by their families. Others clearly demand attention and affection from staff in the nursery or infant school, but we cannot simply assume that these children are therefore emotionally neglected by their parents. In fact, emotionally deprived children may build an invisible barrier thus preventing staff from getting too close, or, as a result of their experiences of rejection, be unwilling to trust the affections of another adult. Mia Kellmer Pringle (1974) suggested that all children have basic needs for love and security, new experiences, praise and recognition, and responsibility. John Bowlby's (1951, 1953) views on maternal deprivation and the consequences of lack of bonding have been challenged, and some of the most recent research suggests that day care for even the youngest children need not be harmful (Melhuish 1991). However, as with the work of many of the great pioneers, Bowlby's work should not be 'thrown out with the bath water', since the refinements to his work in more recent years have pointed to the fact that the quality of the relationships the child experiences are crucial to that child's development. Watt (1990) argues that professionals working with families should be aware of the complex nature of vulnerability and the ways in which we may need to examine our assumptions. She alludes to the problems which could beset children of 'yuppie families', children who experience fleeting parental attention and frequent changes of carer, together with little regard for continuity of experience.

Although emotional abuse is currently gaining more attention, one can appreciate the difficulties in agreeing about the scope of this category. It may be the form of abuse which depends more than any other upon the social group to which those creating the definitions belong, and this in itself can be dangerous. For example, Dahlberg (1991) suggests that the shaping of the children of the 'new middle class' so that they are ready and able to respond to and benefit from changing societal demands, goes hand in hand with unrealistically high expectations of them, which could prove intolerable for many of those children.

Sexual abuse and ritualistic abuse in the UK have been the most difficult for society to come to terms with, so that it was not until May 1986 that a DHSS draft circular included a recommendation that child sexual abuse be included within the child abuse framework. Sexual abuse can include fondling, masturbation, oral sex, anal and vaginal intercourse, exposing children to pornographic materials, videos, sexual sadism and exhibitionism. If the sexual activity is between members of a family, it is labelled incest, although the legal definition applies to sexual intercourse between a man and a woman within the 'prohibited relationships' (Lyon and de Cruz 1990). Some feminists disagree with the 'softening' of the impact of the behaviour by the use of the word 'incest', used instead of 'child rape' in the case of sexual activity between an adult male and his female child relative.

Perhaps the most horrifying facts to come to light concerning child sexual abuse relate to the extent to which it has been occurring in society for many years, and the age at which some children begin to be victimized in this way. The NSPCC (1989) statistics of registered cases of sexual abuse indicate that even babies under one year are abused in this way. Further, between 1983 and 1987, 687 children aged from birth to nine years were registered as sexually abused, and in the 10–16 age group this figure was 855; in other words, for every five teenagers who are abused, approximately four very young and pre-teen children are abused. Those who argue that teenage sexual abuse is the result of a 'Lolita effect' must surely recognize the terrible assumptions they are making about where blame lies. It is not only pubescent girls who are being subjected to this behaviour – largely from adult, or older, male relatives – although girls formed 82 per cent of the reported sexual abuse victims and 78 per cent of that abuse occurred in the girls' own homes.

### Interpreting child abuse statistics

Brian Corby (1990) draws attention to the fact that until recently no national statistics were available, and that the only available data, from the NSPCC, were derived from only 9 per cent of the child population, in those areas where the NSPCC special units kept registers. Corby adds that this information is desperately needed by both practitioners and policy makers, but that one should be cautious of interpreting it. First, it is important to acknowledge that the cases of abuse which reach registration are only 'the tip of the iceberg' (Corby 1990: 305), so that we remain oblivious to the true extent of the ill-treatment suffered by our children. Secondly, the figures cannot demonstrate whether or not violence towards children is more or less prevalent in society than it was a few years ago, because the data refer only to officially recognized abuse. In fact, Corby adds, citing Gelles and Straus (1987), that physical abuse in the USA appears to have declined, but I would caution that one must be wary of assuming that data collected in the USA can be extrapolated to the UK, and further, that one should beware of assuming a decline in reporting to mean a decline in real terms. As one infant teacher told me recently, the staff at her school think that the only form of abuse now considered notable is sexual abuse – so is physical abuse being overlooked? Returning to the NSPCC (1989) statistics, there has been a decline of around 50 per cent in the cases of abuse reported by teachers, and in the past most of these had been physical abuse of pre-school children. Corby (1990) inter-prets the available data and warns that the large increases in over-all reporting of suspected cases of abuse suggest (1) a widening of the definitions, (2) a vast increase in resources (including human resources) and (3) vital training implications.

The statistics can also be used for local authorities to evaluate their own practice, by comparing both registration and de-registration rates with those of other local authorities. Corby (1990: 307) asks:

Why did Rochdale deregister nearly four times as many children as neighbouring Bury in the same year? Why does Bradford have nearly three times as many children on its register as Sheffield, why Liverpool twice as many as Manchester?

Similar discrepancies were noted by Virginia Bottomley, then Minister of State for Health (report in *The Independent*, 27 September 1990), with Lambeth and Liverpool having the highest rates of reported physical abuse (4.3 and 3.8 per 1000 children respectively), and Greenwich and Haringey the highest rates of detected sexual abuse (2.9 and 2.4 per 1000 children respectively, compared with 0.6 for England overall).

Are the differences due to different methods of record-keeping, or other factors? Are some authorities using different criteria for decisions about registration?

## The effects of the Children Act 1989, the 1988 Education Reform Act and Local Authority Policies

The principles underpinning the 1989 Children Act – parental responsibilities; support for families; listening to children; attention to the child's cultural, religious, racial and linguistic background; and interprofessional collaboration – signal a new approach which may be developed into positive and supportive strategies for families where abuse is a potential threat. The ways in which local authorities use resources and develop collaborative strategies will no doubt vary, and interpretation of the definitions and levels of inappropriate treatment of children may depend on those in significant positions within each local authority. Although uniformity may be undesirable, because it may give rise to a 'levelling down' rather than 'up', it is important that workers from different professions and voluntary services come together with each other, and with their counterparts in other local authorities, to share experiences, expertise and ideas. Again, this takes us back to resourcing – schools with tight budgets are unlikely to release teachers for such conferences, let alone find the fees and travel funds. Further, some in the field of education fear that the competition between schools for pupils will mean that issues such as child abuse will be ignored, because of the stigma that might be attached to a school.

In a similar vein, parents and the community at large, unless they already have a trusting relationship with the school staff, may fear that any focus on child abuse could lead to their children being falsely identified as having been abused, and this could result in the removal of pupils to other schools.

There are those who complain (e.g. Campbell and Neill 1990) that the time taken up by the National Curriculum overburdens early years teachers. The focus on the content of the National Curriculum and observations of children relating to the required assessments, may cause teachers to miss signs of potential or real abuse. Additionally, it could be argued that this focus on subject study means personal and social education (PSE) is fast becoming little more than a handful of issues like child protection.

Despite the intention of the Children Act 1989, is the effect of the 1988 Education Reform Act actually countering the demand for closer collaboration between services? Will early years teachers in the UK, who for so long have prided themselves on their attention to the holistic development of children, move away from this style, to one approved of by those who would argue that a teacher should not be a social worker – a teacher's job is to teach? A clearer definition of roles may indeed make life easier. Yet we are faced with the question of what the effects of professional overload will be for those children and families for whom the school could provide the most immediate support. Further, what can be done about the fact that workers have no time to reflect on *why* some children in our society are experiencing abuse?

# ▪ FOUR ▪

# FAMILIES AND VIOLENCE

In Chapter 2, I referred to the myth that has been promulgated concerning a golden age during which everyone lived as a part of an idealized 'family'. The recent census (21 April 1991) highlighted the way in which we distinguish between 'family' and 'household'. The *New Oxford Dictionary* (1909) suggests the family is 'members of a household, parents, children, servants, etc; set of parents and children, or of relations, whether living together or not . . .', though in this day and age few of us would expect to see 'servants' in such a definition.

### Theorizing about the family

The idea that the family is a 'natural' phenomenon is often claimed by those who wish to challenge alternative family forms. However, there is no anthropological or historical evidence to support the idea that one type of family form takes precedence. Abbott (1989) suggests that the evidence we have indicates a variety of structures, often co-existing alongside each other, and that in pre-industrial Britain it is likely that most children lived in households containing other 'kin' as well as their own siblings. The traditional nuclear family is, like childhood, a social construct which is often held up as both the norm and the ideal, perpetuated by many media, from television dramas and advertisements to children's reading schemes.

Some theorists argue that nuclear families exist because they form a vital function in today's society and that this form is predominant because it has been successful. In other words, it suits the society it serves, socializing the young and providing succour and support for the workers (usually the adult males). Despite the divorce rate, most children still experience the nuclear family, and with the rate of remarriage, together with the effects of the 1989 Children Act, many may well divide their lives between two such families.

Feminists theorizing about the family, while acknowledging that the wider aspects of a society reinforce the patriarchal values promulgated by families (Barrett and McIntosh 1982), argue that the

> . . . locus for unequal relations between men and women and adults and children is perceived as lying in 'the family'. As such, the family has become a vital and central symbol to notions of authority, inequality and deference. (Gittins 1985: 58)

Marxists held a negative view of the family, as a tool of the capitalist system, until more recently, when, according to Dahlstrom (1989), it has been argued that the family should not be blamed for contradictions in the capitalist system, since the worker's family provides a resource against life's struggle. Marx and Engels had believed that property relations, not patriarchal relations, were at fault, and although Engels in particular noted the exploitation of women in the 'bourgeois family', they did not think through their notions of the organization of work and leisure as they related to the existing gender division of labour (Gittins 1985).

It may be that we are entering a period when there is no longer an automatic connection between marriage and parenting. The way in which the 1989 Children Act is underpinned by the principle that services should be provided to support families, to keep them together, appears to reinforce the notion of that automatic connection. The other principles of the Act – parental responsibility; joint custody as the automatic response to divorce and separation; the child's interests being paramount and the child's voice being heard – together with conciliation service work and the results of research showing the benefits to children of maintaining contact with both parents, support the idea that parents will, in future, continue their responsibilities for, and relationships with, their children. However, the parents' contract with each other will be terminable.

Research by Dahlstrom (1989) indicates that despite gloomy views about the disappearance of the family and the 'systematic destruction of the nest' (Shorter 1976), the family continues to hold great importance in terms of its functions – subsistence and reproduction. Rather, it is the forms of the family which have altered in Western capitalist societies. Unfortunately, the external demands of life in such a system create contradictions which can be problematic for families; for example, if production and profit are made the ultimate goals of a society, the task of combining employment and parenthood will only be achieved after much thought, time and education, as Rapoport and Moss (1990) demonstrate in their study of Sweden and the UK. A further contradiction is that concerned with efforts to improve the quality of life for families: should these be seen as simply an end in themselves, for families, or as contributing to the national good? Are professionals working with families drafted in to ameliorate conditions for the members of those families (Foster 1988–9), or to ensure the 'policing' of families which might otherwise prove too great a burden on the economy and which, furthermore, may appear to make no contribution to the nation's wealth creation? A third contradiction relates to the current crisis in the UK, that of the decline in the number of school and college leavers available to join the workforce, and the subsequent need for women, including the mothers of small children, to participate in employment. While there is, at a rhetorical level, encouragement for women to continue employment, and in many areas of employment overt equal opportunities policies exist, women still face many unresolved difficulties, such as their being forced to adapt to the 'masculine' nature of the external world, rather than seeing their 'female' values being adopted.

## State intervention

Much of today's debate focuses on the limits of state intervention into the family . . . To what extent is domestic violence or cohabitation a private matter? How much autonomy in child rearing practices should parents be accorded? (Freeman 1983: 1)

Ideologically, the legal system in the UK supports and legitimizes patriarchy (Freeman 1983), not because the rights and duties of husbands and wives are laid down in statutes, but because they are not, and as a result there appears to be a consensus among the judiciary (i.e. lawyers, judges, government bureaucrats) about the nature of family relationships. Tim Eggar, a former Conservative Government Minister of Education, summed up this view by stating: 'I am in politics because I enjoy it . . . My wife and two children are my hobby away from here' (Aitken 1991).

Jane Lewis (1986) debates the extent to which all groupings in society, not just the middle class, have espoused the 'ideal' of the bourgeois family, and, far from resenting state assistance to (or interference in) their families, as writers such as Lasch (1977) have suggested, working-class families resent the manner of delivery and stigmatization resulting from the involvement of professional agencies. However, many families do need, and feel able to accept, help to overcome complex problems of disadvantage. According to Coffield (1983), these problems of disadvantage stem from a mixture of socio-economic processes and family modes of action.

Lewis (1986) suggests that changes in attitudes towards poverty, gender roles and state functions have resulted in different policies and practices at different times during this century. During the first decade, although working-class families shared the bourgeois family ideal, there were not sufficient funds to live according to the demands of that ideal. In families where women were paid for work, whether that be work within the home or without, the women were pitied and the men scorned, as either inadequate providers or wasteful and neglectful drunkards. Eugenicists believed that the poor inherited this tendency, as well as vices which they suggested went hand-in-hand with pauperism. It is thought that this type of belief led to families being split up when their dire circumstances caused them to enter the workhouse. Thus, there was a kind of 'policing' to reinforce the bourgeois family ideal.

After the Second World War, a similar popular movement to reinstate the family occurred, as a result of fears about dislocations caused by the war itself and, for example, children's evacuation. Radio psychologists and doctors broadcast advice, all based on underlying assumptions of the supremacy and naturalness of the bourgeois family. While failure in the earlier part of the century had been attributed to fathers, it was now attributed to mothers. The impact of the work of Bowlby (1953) and Winnicott (1964) had many effects, including the NSPCC making a link between children's well-being and full-time motherhood (Lewis 1986). The advent of the Welfare State caused social commentators to believe that poverty had been eradicated and family failure was now the result of personal inadequacy. In other words, the victims were still being blamed, the rationalizations about the causes had simply been changed.

The mood of more recent years has resulted from the long period of government by the New Right. The view that too much support by the state causes learned helplessness has led to the formation of pressure groups calling for more policies which 'help' families undertake their responsibilities for the young, the sick and the elderly, but do not actually take over. This is apparent in the restrictions on public provision of nursery education and day care, and the view expressed by various government ministers that child care is a private matter. Here we see the whole New Right model of society coming together – self-reliance, voluntary work and private enterprise – in which the state has a much reduced responsibility.

While one might wish to argue that such policies have hardly been based on the needs of children, as Lewis (1986) points out, this has so far never been the case. During the 1940s, the years of the founding of the Welfare State, a handful of politicians reiterated the words of Eleanor Rathbone (1924) and attempted to argue for a system which was to be based on human welfare, but which would not be premised upon the assumption that women who became mothers would automatically quit the labour force. What is unfortunate about this failure, particularly in the light of the more recent New Right policies, is that a view of a society so tightly defined according to the bourgeois ideal fails to recognize the dangers in the system (e.g. see Anderson 1988). As Joan Cooper (1987–8: 19) points out: 'Family is an emotional sanctuary or an emotional hell and except in our minds and personal experience, it defies definition.'

## Violence in families or violent families?

When *Dangerous Families* (Dale *et al.* 1986) was published, it created something of a stir with both its title and its cover photograph of a child, slumped in a rather rag-doll-like pose, in a small armchair. The emotive photograph was criticized because it portrayed a child looking very much the epitome of a 'victim' rather than a 'survivor'. I do not intend here to enter into the semiotic debate about the problems of using certain photographs of children on the covers of publications (or in charity advertisements), nor to discuss the effects of the image of victim rather than survivor, other than to suggest that such semiotic explorations could be important and fruitful approaches to our own professional and personal development, our awareness of attitudes towards children, abuse and childhood as a concept.

The title, on the other hand, was considered to be problematic because it was thought to give the impression that there are certain families which are pathologically dangerous. Some critics felt that this type of focus would lead to a denial of the possibility that child abuse, especially physical abuse and neglect, could be perpetrated by any one of us, as a result of ideological or contextual factors that may put families under tremendous stress. Dale *et al.* (1986) argue that it is family dynamics which produces the inappropriate behaviour, and that if parents can be enabled to acknowledge their own relationship difficulties, they can come to recognize their inappropriate behaviour in relation to their children. Once this happens, children who have been removed from the home may be returned and the possibility of re-abuse is apparently reduced, although Dale *et al.* seem pessimistic about the success rate. The difficulty is that such a focus, while appearing quite feasible, may result in the blaming of victims and may overlook other factors which complicate the issue. Additionally, responsibility for the abuse is sited in the family, rather than with the abuser.

What we need to ask is, why and how do members of some families experience violence? Writers and researchers often specialize in investigations into one form of family violence, whether the physical or sexual abuse of children, aggression towards wives, or, occasionally, aggression towards the elderly or husbands. In stating that family abuse is an abuse of power, Finkelhor (1983: 18) adds that this 'is not even the full story . . . Abuse tends to gravitate toward the relationships of greatest power differential.' In other words, those with the greatest power in a family group will be most likely to pick on the weakest member in relation to themselves. This is, Finkelhor suggests, true whatever form of abuse of power one examines. Physical abusers of children, while roughly 50 per cent men and 50 per cent women, in terms of actual number of incidents reported, are overwhelmingly male adults, if the frequency of incidence is calculated as a rate for the amount of time spent with the children. Furthermore, it is the youngest children who are the most vulnerable to this type of abuse. Similarly, according to reported statistics, the sexual abuse of children is perpetrated overwhelmingly by males – whether adult or not, they are bigger and stronger than their victims, as are wife abusers.

Gelles (1973), having noted the fact that many male perpetrators seemed to be rather pathetic and ineffectual adults in the public milieu, suggested that this may account for the abuse of power within the family, as a way of compensating for their perceived lack of power elsewhere. Finkelhor (1983) reports that mothers often become violent towards their children when they feel they have lost control over their own lives, or over the lives of their children. Washburne (1983) has argued that workers will not influence the numbers of mothers physically abusing their children until women have true equality in society, because their behaviour results from their feelings of frustration and impotence within society.

As well as those factors which lead to poor self-esteem, such as a deterioration in a relationship with a partner or lack of warm relationships with others who cherish the abuser, other factors which may predispose parents to become abusers are (a) having been subjected to abuse themselves as children, (b) incorrect perceptions of the child and (c) alcohol or drug abuse.

First, the experience of being abused may mean that violent or inappropriate behaviour has been internalized as a normal way for a parent to behave, or it may have caused such a feeling of worthlessness that mature relationships cannot be achieved. In a way, this latter point is also implicated in the misperception of the victim – a baby's crying may be interpreted as a dislike and lack of love for the perpetrator, thus sustaining their belief in themselves as unlovable.

Finkelhor (1988: 22), reviewing the research on family violence, suggests that 'family violence researchers are still far from agreement about how best to explain the different kinds of family violence. They have much greater consensus, however, about who is at risk.' He then stresses that the studies fail to confirm the stereotyped notion of abusers of children as disturbed and malevolent people. They are 'parents caught in highly stressful, unsupportive circumstances who have ineffective and unrealistic behaviours and attitudes surrounding child care' (p. 22). They tend to be low-income, teenage parents, parents without partners, parents with unwanted children, often socially isolated, or having a child with special needs because of illness or disability. These risk factors have been used in some areas in the USA to identify potential abusers and in teenagers' parenthood education programmes. Sceptics might argue that such a checklist merely focuses attention on particular groups in society, so that there will be high identification rates in those groups, confirming the belief that these are the facts. Meanwhile, physical abuse, emotional abuse and neglect in more affluent circles may go unnoticed.

Sexual abuse risk factors have proved even more problematic. Retrospective studies have yielded more information than is possible from concurrent research. Finkelhor (1988) states the now well-known fact that children are more likely to be sexually abused by a stepfather than a father, and this abuse is most likely to occur at a time when the parents' relationship is in difficulties. Some theorists are now suggesting that one important factor is the building of a close relationship during the child's babyhood, through everyday care and contact, because this appears to act as a preventative measure to the likelihood of sexual abuse. There could be a variety of explanations, ranging from the fact that it may be the case that fathers who become involved in baby care are unlikely to have rigid, strongly patriarchal attitudes towards their families (a factor which researchers suggest is prevalent in abusive situations; Finkelhor 1983), to the development of appropriate nurturing through understanding, based on knowledge about babies and children.

### Putting theories about the family into practice

When the Seebohm Committee (DHSS 1968) debated their remit to explore a family model for the social services, its members realized the difficulties involved, and after recognizing that they could only make sense of their task by considering the needs of generations of families and childless couples and those living alone, they felt it necessary to argue for a service which became universal, but 'family based'.

Perhaps the idea of agonizing over a definition of 'family' appears an irrelevant academic pastime; however, it is important to recognize the effects any chosen definition will have on policies and on their implementation. For example, some countries have developed policies which are far more supportive to whole ranges of alternative family structures, than have other countries. The International Labour Office in Geneva characterizes the UK as a country with no, or few, overt Family Policies, whereas France, a country concerned to foster an upswing in its devastated population after the two World Wars, developed many positive policies to encourage families which included a number of children. Other countries, such as Sweden, have a strong sense of the responsibility of all members of the state towards the next generation. As a result, levels of day-care provision for children under school age are very high in number, and of high quality. Similarly, the former East Germany offered preschool provision for all children aged over one year, and leave from work for mothers with a child under that age, because the government decided babies needed close, one-to-one interactions for optimal development.

Two countries which turned from the close-knit family because it was thought too oppressive, the former Soviet Union and Israel, have both experienced a resurgence of the desire to live in, and spend private time with, a family. Sommerville (1982) claims that in those countries in which the government encourages a variety of social bonds by offering some support to families, sharing child-rearing and presumably also the care of the elderly, life in families is thriving in a way which is not happening in those societies where support is haphazard.

### So are families best for children?

Suransky (1982: 15) argues that:

> . . . childhood is left barren by excessive psychologizing . . . The struggle for the democratization of the family and the elimination of sex hierarchy and privilege can only be successfully waged in a grounded commitment to the children as well as to the adults involved. Self-actualization, without corresponding familial and social commitment by both men and women, merely continues the 'script' of domination previously mapped by men as the dominant cartography of an individualistic ethos of interpersonal relations.

Schaffer (1990), reviewing research on the traditional family and its importance to children's well-being, stresses the fact that there is fairly unanimous agreement, despite the diversity of the research studies involved, that alternative lifestyles with children – such as single parenthood, working mothers, role reversal, same-sex couples – are not necessarily harmful to children. It is often the secondary effects of some of these family forms, such as poverty in the case of single parenthood or poor quality day care in the case of maternal employment, which cause ill-effects, not the life-styles *per se* (Tunnard 1987–8). Schaffer does add a note of caution, however, in that some of the evidence he uses comes from studies undertaken in other countries, where attitudes to alternative patterns may be less censorious than in British society. As I pointed out in 1990, it may be the attitudes prevalent in a society which do actual damage because of the resulting behavioural effects. McLean (1991) argues that the relationship between attitudes and behaviours may not be straightforward, but attitudes are determinants and components of actions. What seems to be crucial for the well-being of children, according to Schaffer's (1990) conclusions from his survey, is the quality of the relationships they encounter, rather than the structure of the family.

Dahlberg (1991) argues that recent research in European countries has shown parent–child relationships to be changing, moving from a value system in which children are expected to love and respect their authoritarian parents *per se*, to one in which the relationship is characterized by love, friendship, democracy and autonomy. Further, parents are attempting to equate their parenting skills with those of trained professionals who work with young children. This is partly because they believe the experts to know 'best' and partly because they are afraid too great a discrepancy between home values and preschool or school group values, may confuse the developing child.

There seem to be two major patterns of child–parent relationships: (1) the child as 'project', where parents have very high expectations of their child, and attempt to both shape the child and to structure the child's experiences; (2) 'child as immediate presence' (Dahlberg, ibid.), where the child is regarded as a *child*, given rules and guidelines, but left more to get on with their life ('they will grow up soon enough'). While both sets of parents are attempting to respond sympathetically to the needs of their children, the 'new middle class' more frequently adopt the 'child as project' model, and, in so doing, prepare their children to adapt to varying demands and conditions in society. Though this may mean such children are advantaged, they may also be stressed by parental expectations.

Professionals working with young children and their families need to be aware of such changes, currents and expectations in society. Their analysis of the ways in which these pressures affect family life will be crucial to the ways in which they interact with different families and their ability to work sensitively. Further, they need an awareness of the models of adult–child relationships they themselves adopt; if what they demonstrate is unattainable for some parents, is this good practice or the imposition of white, middle-class values? What should their strategies be?

# FIVE

# WHY DOES ABUSE OCCUR?

In Chapter 4, many points were raised to argue that factors like poverty and stress contribute to the likelihood of child abuse. However, it is important to acknowledge that there are a number of theories which have been proposed as possible explanations for the abuse of children, and in this chapter I present those theories and some of the counter-arguments. The main points to bear in mind, however, are: that no one theory seems able to explain all forms of abuse; that the theories are merely tentative, and we have not prevented abuse by their application; the theory, or theories, which different people espouse are likely to be a reflection of their general attitudes and values, and their political beliefs about society, people and life.

This book is concerned with the role of teachers in protecting children from abuse, largely abuse that occurs in the home environment or the 'home' of a person known to the child. Additionally, however, it is important to acknowledge that there have been cases of child abuse by teachers, other staff and strangers – within the school environment – so again these aspects must be borne in mind when considering some of the theories.

The theories could be divided into three broad categories:

- *biological* – that is, the causes are thought to stem from our 'animal' make-up, or physiological factors within our bodies;
- *psychological or sociological* – these theories attempt to provide

explanations for abuse which are derived from learning theories, or cultural factors, etc.;

■ *political* – these theories posit the idea that power imbalances are at the root of child abuse.

## Biological theories

Using Bowlby's (1951) ideas about the necessity for babies to attach to a mother figure (preferably the 'natural' mother), these theorists have argued that when adults have not had secure attachments in their own early childhood, they are unable to bond with their own offspring and may therefore abuse them. Other theorists have adapted Dawkins' (1976) *selfish gene* view of the behaviour of adult males. In their struggle to ensure that their own genes are passed on to many children and in order to ensure their survival, males are given licence, according to this adapted theory, to impregnate as many females as possible and to damage or kill any earlier offspring from previous mates.

On the whole, such theories seem a sad indictment of the human race. Surely, the numerous step-parents who do not maltreat their stepchildren, the numerous mothers who love and cherish their children, despite their own unhappy early experiences, provide the lie to these theories. Cannot human beings learn to overcome such difficulties, and is there not now sufficient evidence (e.g. Clarke and Clarke 1976) to demonstrate that early experience is not critical? (Critical here is the psychologists' meaning of the word, i.e. once for all necessity.)

## Psychological and sociological theories

During the early years of his work, Sigmund Freud found that many of the women who came to him for treatment of their neuroses told of abuse by fathers, or other powerful adult males in their family circles. Perhaps as a result of pressure from society, Freud altered the explanations for his findings, suggesting that as children these women had fantasized about the men in question, and they had not grown out of this immature stage in their development (see Corby 1989). Psychoanalysts continued for many years basing their work on the assumption that sexual abuse did not happen in the 'respectable' families from which their own and Freud's patients came. However, Alice Miller (1987, 1991), the Swiss psychoanalyst, has argued that telling victims they have imagined the abuse causes further damage. What is crucial to survivors and their later ability to cope is their experience of being loved and accepted by someone. Miller uses the life of Adolf Hitler as a prime example of a child who had no such person, no such experience of being valued.

The main contributions this theory has made to the field of protection work are: the need for that positive relationship; the long-term damage which abusive relationships can cause; and the need for therapy for most victims of abuse.

*Learning theory*, in particular behaviourism, suggests that abuse is learned. Thus, if children experience only this type of treatment at the hands of adults, they will in turn become abusers. The theory also rests on the assumption that the abuse brings some kind of reward and reinforcement of these behaviours.

The idea that some families are 'dysfunctional', that illness is actually caused by poor *family dynamics*, by misunderstandings due to poor communications and contradictory 'messages', has been put forward by psychiatrists and social workers from the field of mental health. According to this theory, family members will wreak their revenge for their own feelings of frustration, inadequacy, loneliness, etc., on other family members. One member, usually a child, may be picked out as the family scapegoat, blamed for all that is wrong. Families will be encouraged to become more outward looking, developing relationships with others outside the family circle, because this offers not only relief from the intense relationships of the abusive web, but also models of living together which are not 'dysfunctional'.

Sociological theories come under three headings. First, there is the *ecological* sociological theory, which was used in much of the discussion in the previous chapter. This theory suggests that a variety of factors within the environment, such as a lack of opportunities for appropriate parenting skills to be learned, poverty and stress, and a lack of community support, are to blame for the resort to abuse of children.

*Social cultural theories* are based on the premise that childrearing patterns passed on and accepted by a cultural or subcultural group may be defined by others as abusive. This theory requires us to make childrearing a topic of public debate, to discuss, for example, the fact that while most four-year-olds in the UK are smacked every week because it is thought to be an appropriate way of dealing with four-year-olds' behaviour and supposed lack of ability to understand explanations, this would not be accepted in Sweden. In the UK, there is a high level of tolerance of abusive behaviour because we, as a society, allow smacking to be part of a parent's repertoire. Indeed, some might say, we even think it natural that parents should hit their children.

Perhaps the most important aspect of this theory is the way it highlights the position of black (Afro-Caribbean) and Asian families and the ways in which their childrearing practices may be stereotyped by social workers, health visitors, and so on. Additionally, white professionals may be reluctant to intervene if they feel they will be subjected to the charge of racism. This signals a need for all services to evaluate their philosophical underpinning in relation to anti-racist theory and practice.

*Social structural theory* is based on the premise that most abuse occurs in the most disadvantaged groups in society, and therefore the whole of society is to blame and should make amends by changing access to material necessities and to power. The problems with this theory are that it fails to take account of the way in which disadvantaged groups in our society are 'policed' – we simply cannot be certain that abuse is not occurring among the more advantaged groups. Furthermore, since those with the power are those who define what constitutes abuse, there may be forms of behaviour which others believe inappropriate but which do not receive the label abuse, yet which could affect some, or all, of the children involved (e.g. early entry to boarding school).

Although this theory has been grouped with the sociological and psychological theories of child abuse, it could in fact be included in the next section, as a political theory, since its proponents would require a political solution.

### Political theories

Patriarchy is the cause of abusive behaviour to those with less power, according to *feminist theory*. Writers such as Mary MacLeod and Esther Saraga (1987, 1988), Emily Driver (1989) and Audrey Droisen (1989) have suggested that child abuse and child pornography cannot be eradicated from our society while we maintain a system in which adult males are vested with such power over other members of that society, namely, women and children.

Eileen Vizard (1987) argues that feminist theory cannot explain male abuse of boys, but this seems to be an incorrect assumption on her part, since feminist theory is predicated upon power being held by adult males, and thus there is no contradiction in the view that exploitation of smaller or younger males (i.e. males with less power) is perpetrated by those with more. Similarly, critics have suggested that the theory is incapable of explaining the physical abuse of children by their mothers. I would argue that this is possible, since it is likely that women who abuse their own children, whether physically or emotionally, are placed in a position where they are relatively powerless compared with other members of society, and they are thus accorded so little status they give vent to their frustrations by acting aggressively towards their children. Possibly as a result of feeling that they themselves are undervalued, mothers are incapable of valuing their own children, despite the fact that their children may actually mean a great deal to them. There is also the argument that society expects them to control and discipline their children, so they do so in this way.

A theory based on assertions about *children's rights* are made by two groups, according to Michael Freeman (1983). He identifies one group as 'liberators', people who argue that children should be treated in just the same ways as adults, that they should have the right to vote, to financial independence, to live where they choose, to freedom from physical punishment and sexual freedom. Against this, there is the argument that, in general, parents seek to protect their children while they are immature, and that the idea of implementing the proposals of the liberators would be very difficult – for example, at what age should children be free to choose where they live? The second group, the 'protectionists', believe that children should be entitled to 'welfare rights' (basic human rights such as adequate food, shelter, etc.) and to protection from exploitation. The Children Act 1989 would appear to meet the demands of the protectionists but not the liberators.

Kitzinger (1990) argues that a protectionist stance can impose further restrictions on children, and this is symbolized by the bars of the prison-like structures behind which survivors depict themselves in drawings. She suggests that theorists are wrong to assume child abuse is simply an abuse of power. Instead, she argues, abuse is a function of childhood as an institution, as it is currently lived in our society, because of the existence and maintenance of power differentials between adults and children, and between bigger/older children and smaller/younger ones.

## Applying theories to individual cases of child abuse

In our work, we are always attempting to link theory with practice, to relate a real-life situation to possible theoretical models which may provide generalizations. Some of the theories locate the causes of abuse within a single person, some within individual families, some within sections of society and others within society as a whole. It is apparent that some forms of abuse are more likely to be the result of a combination of these effects, others a single causative element. Some of the theories will be attractive to particular groups of workers because they offer fruitful courses of action, attainable goals, whereas others appear more difficult to apply, or less amenable to short-term solutions.

As I stated earlier, the theories we espouse may well reflect our own experiences of the world, our own political viewpoint. If we believe that the 'natural' nuclear family is 'the' context in which children should be brought up, then we may be unable to support feminist theory, or the liberationists' theories emphasizing children's rights, or the sociological theories – we are perhaps most likely to espouse the biological theories, or the psychodynamic and family dysfunction theories, which lay blame at the feet of nature, badness or madness. In exploring which theories we find most feasible, we should perhaps ask ourselves why we have chosen one and rejected another, since we may learn much about our own attitudes to abuse, while at the same time being forced to recognize that we are unwilling to accept other ways of thinking, and we must be articulate about our reasons for and against particular theories.

# SIX

# RESEARCHING CHILD ABUSE

I have already pointed out the difficulties practitioners and researchers have had in comparing the definitions of the various types of child abuse, and the difficulties which have arisen from this, and other factors, concerning statistical records. On an international scale, the problem is even more complex, because cultural factors determine what does and does not constitute abuse and neglect, and cultural factors will have influenced the legal framework of the country concerned, so that behaviour which is seen as meriting criminal prosecution in one country will not necessarily do so in another, even if the behaviour is censured. Although the UN Convention on Children's Rights, which some developing countries' representatives found Euro/US-centric, may produce greater uniformity of recognition of abuses to children in ratifying countries, there may still be problems of interpretation.

It may be that one society sees an abusive act as indicative of illness, or stress, needing treatment or support, rather than imprisonment. Not only will the cultural climate have determined the laws themselves, but it will have engendered the system in which certain members of that society are deemed qualified to make decisions concerning the abuse, and the way in which those people interpret the law may well reflect the values prevalent in their own, usually elite, group.

An illustration of this would be the group who constitute judges in the UK. The great majority of these are mature, white males from a very privileged background. Considering the fact that it is only recently that gender issues began to be recognized as important in all areas of life, it is hardly surprising that some judges have shown themselves to be unaware of their own male supremacism. In a case where a father of a 12-year-old girl was being tried for incest, the judge argued that there were mitigating circumstances: the man's pregnant wife had denied him sexual intercourse, so he had turned to the daughter. While this may be a particularly extreme example, it is indicative of the underlying indoctrination endemic in our society relating to what is 'natural' human behaviour. It is within this climate that UK researchers are attempting to probe.

This chapter will deal with research issues generally; Chapter 6, research into physical and emotional abuse and neglect; Chapter 7 will deal with sexual and ritualistic abuse. Here I wish to examine some of the issues surrounding abuse which have made it a particularly difficult area for researchers, and those interprofessional issues highlighted by research, because child abuse and protection require particularly high-quality liaison. It is important for us to examine these two areas, since teachers need the knowledge provided by research to inform their work and procedures, and, additionally, teachers are part of the multi-professional network whose ability to operate effectively can so influence the lives of the children concerned (Hazell 1987).

## Research into professional roles and relationships

Teachers who have had no training in child protection work, nor even training in some of the more obvious practical aspects of interprofessional liaison such as case conferences, would probably be the first to recognize and sympathize with the difficulties encountered arising from a lack of knowledge of the roles of others – in particular, they may well have no real understanding of where the boundaries of their own responsibilities lie.

During the investigation into the death of Heidi Koseda, the Hillingdon Area Review Committee found 'an alarming lack of knowledge of the roles of the professionals involved' (Croale 1986). A 1982 study of inquiry reports into children's deaths included the statement that 'agency functions are to a very large extent shaped, if not actually determined by the law' (DHSS 1982: 5), and it continued by pointing out that in some cases basic training may include similar strands but the objectives of the agency for which one works may dictate the way in which that training is translated into practice, with different professionals having different parts to play in any given situation. The problems which arise as a result of a lack of role definition and role understanding is a frequent feature of child protection crises, including those in Cleveland and the Orkney Islands. When one stops to consider the number of agencies that could be involved (e.g. health visitors, doctors, social workers, teachers, police, NSPCC workers, lawyers, education welfare officers, psychologists, youth and community workers, voluntary agency representatives such as playgroup supervisors), it is hardly surprising that such confusion arises.

First, there is the issue of whether someone from a particular background has any knowledge of their own role and that of the other professionals involved; secondly, what is their personal knowledge and value base concerning child abuse and protection; thirdly, in what way is each contributor able to cope with his or her workload and is he or she supported by adequate management systems and back-up?

It seems likely that at a time when social workers and teachers feel their professions are undervalued and feel pressurized by the implementation of various pieces of legislation, or by cutbacks, there will be little time to allow for what may seem the less direct implications of child protection work. Any available training time and funding will be focused on 'crisis' responses – for example, to legislation such as the 1988 Education Reform Act and the Children Act 1989 – rather than longer-term development of closer liaison and inter-agency understanding.

The very act of becoming involved in multi-agency work is one which increases the stress in one's working life. Research into the levels of stress among workers whose roles involved high frequencies of placatory interactions with a range of different people, some of whom were in conflict with each other, showed that they were likely to suffer from acute occupational stress (Mettlin and Woelfel 1974; Cooper and Payne 1980). This was apparently particularly true of those whose roles demanded they cross, or blur, boundaries related to their own organization and the outside world or other agencies. In other words, social workers – and teachers whose work involves them in interactions with children, parents, the community and other professionals and volunteers – need to be aware of the potential for increased stress inherent in this role development.

That this type of development is required by the 1989 and that it may well appear simple and straightforwal for teachers and others to come together, glosses ove nature of multi-professional interaction.

While one would expect that networking as a form of support, whether inter- or intra-agency, should alleviate stress, it should be added that this aspect of support needs to be overtly recognized. If it is not, the relationships created can end up becoming an additional source of strain, because they engender feelings of guilt at making sure one performs one's fair share of the work, and doing it to a high standard (e.g. see Baker 1988).

A further reason for improving the understanding of the roles of others involved in multi-professional work is confidence. A number of studies and events have called into question social workers' confidence in the ability of medical practitioners to diagnose physical, and especially sexual, abuse (e.g. Hobbs and Wynne 1986; Roberts 1986; Dyer 1987; Sharron 1987).

The perceptions held by colleagues from other professions will be formed as a result of many factors, but the likelihood of their being positive will, at present, depend upon their knowledge of that profession, its status within society and personal interactions based on personalities, rather than any carefully structured mechanisms for those liaisons to occur. Research undertaken by the NSPCC in the 1970s (Castle 1976) into the effectiveness of case conferences, raised issues related to perceptions of one professional group by another. In particular, medical members were thought to be assuming 'omnipotence' (ibid.: 12) and in some cases it was felt that despite case conference recommendations, each agency would revert to 'doing its own thing' (ibid.: 12), although case conferences were thought to be contributing to improvements in inter-agency cooperation and communication. Research on teamwork in industry (see Chapter 14) may hold some clues about the ways in which the initial make-up of teams and the delineation of roles could be improved upon in the caring professions. The

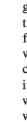

problem with the current organization is that even if we knew what qualities are needed to fill a 'gap' in a team, there are no mechanisms for ensuring that the person selected, usually purely by dint of being in a particular place at a particular time, will have the necessary qualities.

Headteachers questioned by Byron (1987) were generally positive about case conferences, although some expressed reservations, uch as too much emphasis on the needs of parents, as opposed to the children, and the time-consuming nature of the task.

Confidentiality is an issue which some agency representatives feel is open to misuse, and the fact that some of the professions involved have a code of conduct, while others do not, needs discussion and clarification.

The status of different workers within society, the fact that some are more likely to have a greater representation of women, or are subject to vertical segregation, with the majority of senior posts held by men, may again be the cause of difficulties. As a result, the sensitivity and skill of the person chairing case conferences is crucial, and perhaps this is most vital when parents are part of that case conference group.  Shemmings and Thoburn's (1990) research on parental attendance at case conferences argues that it is possible that the conferences themselves are expected to fulfil too many functions. Again, the importance of the expertise of the chairperson is stressed. In particular, the chairperson should ensure that everyone is heard and, especially when parents are present, that even difficult and painful observations can still be made. Shemmings and Thoburn (1990) also comment that many case conferences are extremely time-consuming, because too much detail about future plans relating to the work of certain key professionals is explored. This could be better discussed in broad terms and left to this smaller team to work out later. Additionally, they found that where a case conference was well conducted, a considerable amount of earlier planning work and involvement with the family had been carried out prior to the conference taking place.

 Blyth and Milner (1990) discuss the complex nature of inter-professional liaison. Hope for the future seems to hang on the development of good working relationships between workers from different agencies, yet they point out that 'paradoxically, effective inter-agency communication may be impeded by ostensibly "good" working relationships' (p. 201). This can occur when 'too-cosy links' have generated 'collusion rather than cooperation'. The need for us to be confident enough, trusting enough, in our relationships with other workers to allow us to accept differences of opinion without feeling a loss of status is central – each person involved has to ask themselves whether they are acting 'in the child's best interests', and how they have interpreted these. Blyth and Milner (1990) make the point that social workers may have adjusted their standards as to what constitutes acceptable levels of parenting, while teachers, exposed to a wider range of children's experience, may hold different expectations.

Not least among the sensitive areas involved in inter-agency work is that of 'territory'. If cooperation means some sort of surrendering of either power or resources, the groups involved may expect a 'payoff' (Homan 1958). Greater inter-agency collaboration means laying bare one's own professional group's systems and strategies, and this increases the organization's vulnerability to evaluation and scrutiny by outsiders (Weissman *et al.* 1983). Add to that the accusations of 'vested interest' in maintaining certain roles because they are powerful as a means of protecting a profession, closing ranks and secrecy become inevitable. Similarly, 'buck passing' as a way of avoiding damage to one's own profession can be a hazard and not 'in the best interests of children'.

At a very basic level, the ways in which geographical areas are divided up by different departments (as a headteacher at one school, I was involved in interprofessional liaison work involving three social services offices) creates complications, and this will become even more complicated post-ERA, when children may come to a school from outside the old 'catchment area'.

## Researching controversial issues and sensitive aspects of interpersonal relations

The difficulties posed by indefinite, changing or disputed definitions of types of abuse is one of the major problems for both researchers and those wishing to use research findings. A further very real problem for researchers in this field has been the frustration of research ideas due to a lack of funding. Research in the USA, in contrast with Britain, has been quite generously funded. Corby (1987: 11) argues that in the UK:

> . . . very little attention has been given to developing resources for treating or helping families where abuse is suspected – the focus has been almost entirely on improving the system for detecting and managing cases and reliance has been placed on existing resources. Similarly there has been little direct research into child abuse work and related issues – to some extent the findings of public inquiries have served this function. It is as if there has been a reluctance to focus on child abuse because

it is considered to be too narrow a topic in itself. One of the consequences of this is that we are woefully ignorant about certain aspects of the subject, the most glaring example of this being with regard to the extent of the problem.

As far as the education field goes, there has been almost no research whatsoever. To some extent, this may be the result of a lack of research funding, but it is apparent that probing this field may also be unwelcome, owing to fears about adverse publicity.

While one may have some sympathy with such protection, it is hardly the way for a profession to move forward or to learn. Young teachers in training are anxious because they are unable to find the kinds of information they would like, even though they acknowledge that every case will be unique, and that research literature and theories inform experience but do not replace it.

## Ethics and research

One of the reasons why teachers' leaders may wish to protect them from exposure through research may have arisen because of earlier work on less sensitive topics which has led to pain for those involved – how much stronger the desire to prevent a similar occurrence when the focus is potentially such an explosive and damaging one for all concerned. It means that researchers in this field are even more bound than others to follow strict codes of confidentiality and anonymity. I would argue for the use of feminist research/democratic research methods because those 'being researched' maintain 'ownership' of the material they contribute; they are seen as partners in the research process and their viewpoint is faithfully portrayed. Most importantly, they really are 'subjects', not 'objects', in the research project.

In some cases, research into child abuse could be seen as having potential to cause further damage to the survivors, and further ethical dimensions creep in when one begins to consider research which uses 'control groups' and 'experimental groups', since this might imply the allocation of certain children to a group receiving no therapy or support, for example, so as to effect a comparison with the progress of those children who did receive these. The only way to explore such effects would be through naturally occurring groupings of this type, and since those not receiving support may come from a more impoverished social services area, or a totally different socio-economic background to those living in an area where help is at hand, whatever happens the results would be dependent upon a wide range of factors for which there would be little hope of adjusting the variables involved.

Perhaps the largest stumbling block to any research of this topic is the very nature of the area of life under scrutiny. Life within families in the UK has long been held to be private, and until the re-emergence of campaigns for women's rights, it was a taboo subject, with sexual abuse being the most taboo.

Sexuality in relation to children is probably the most taboo of all, and by this I do not mean adult–child sex. What I mean is that society finds it hard to accept the idea that children are sexual beings, despite the fact that childhood sexuality is not the same as adult sexual behaviour. What is worrying, however, is the fact that in our society this innocent sexuality is often exploited and overlaid with current adult preoccupations about sex – sex as dominance, sex as a commodity, and so on. What starts as natural curiosity (Goldman and Goldman 1982) may become the sexist harassment of schoolgirls. Boys' attempts to look up girls' skirts, making embarrassing remarks, and so on, begin very early. Advertisers frequently use young children in certain poses and clothing that would be sexually provocative in a woman (Ennew 1986).

Because many adults feel that young children will be damaged by sex education, losing their childhood innocence, children are often kept in ignorance for far too long. The research of Goldman and Goldman (1988) has shown that children have already acquired knowledge about sexual behaviour and language – or which behaviour and language must be avoided – by the age of five, and they argue that in those countries where children are properly educated about sexuality, children are well able to cope with any questions of morality which may arise.

In a similar way, we have to ask if we live in a society which avoids conflict and issues arising from aggressive behaviour, whether manifested in physical or emotional unkindness, or through being neglectful of another's needs. In school, personal and social education provides a forum for debating such issues, and some teachers believe it is in this context that child abuse should be discussed – yet how are we to develop the evaluation and research to make conclusions on its effectiveness?

Reports from the USA (Gough 1991) indicate that child protection programmes have been used in schools, yet they have had little, if any, positive effect on the rates of child abuse, and it may be that they end up damaging the children because they are left feeling that they have failed to put into practice the techniques they were taught, and that therefore the abuse was their own fault. All we know from the UK (Webster 1991) is that some schools have attempted to use such programmes before staff have become totally confident with either the materials involved or their own expertise.

Taking a wide view of the whole field of child abuse and protection research, it seems likely that we have not begun to think properly about what questions we should be asking; nor, perhaps, do we have research methods which are capable of yielding truly reliable information about abuse. In part, this is due to attitudes in society and secrecy, and in part is a response to the slow rate of attitudinal change. Additionally, there are complications that arise from differing definitions of what constitutes abuse. Perhaps we are too preoccupied with tinkering with the system as it currently exists, rather than asking ourselves some fundamental questions about our society as a whole, how the weak are treated, questions about ownership, about power and politics. But if research could throw light onto those inequalities and their effects, we might begin to rebuild rather than tinker.

# SEVEN

# RESEARCHING PHYSICAL ABUSE, EMOTIONAL ABUSE AND NEGLECT

## Research into physical abuse

The 1948 Children Act, passed by a Labour government, called for a Children's Committee to be set up in each local authority, and a Children's Officer to be appointed. This attempt to bring together the *ad hoc* services available to children could have been the catalyst to wider recognition of child abuse, particularly in the light of the Monckton Report, which detailed the events leading to the death by starvation and physical injury of 12-year-old Denis O'Neill, by his foster parents. Sir Walter Monckton conducted the inquiry, and in his conclusions he criticized the two local authorities concerned and suggested that their role in the care and protection of children should be clarified.

Despite early work in the USA, such as that by Dr John Caffey in the mid-1940s (Caffey 1946), alerting colleagues to his findings of X-ray evidence of earlier multiple fractures in the bodies of young children brought to hospital as a result of subdural haematoma (blood clotting under the skull), it was not for another 18 years that injuries which doctors had attributed to brittle bones began to be seen as potentially the result of cruelty. Griffiths and Moynihan (1963) quoted the 1962 American paper by Dr Henry Kempe and his colleagues (1962) and the label the 'battered baby syndrome' became accepted. Subsequent letters to the *British Medical Journal* demonstrated the suspicions many GPs already had.

As we shall see, one of the problems which has impeded child protection against all forms of abuse is the veil of self-imposed silence surrounding taboos about the family–state divide and the status of childhood in the UK. Further, the initiation of recognition of abuse in the UK by the medical profession, rather than welfare, social or education professionals, was probably responsible to some extent for the difficulties, since the principle of confidentiality meant that doctors, nurses and health visitors were reluctant to use any information publicly, and, in any case, they were especially disinclined to face the idea that families they knew could commit such acts. At that time, the prevailing view, spearheaded by two forensic pathologists, was that the authorities should declare a 'war against abusive parents' (Parton, 1985: 56).

More recent researchers (see Vondra and Toth 1989) have begun to recognize that, where earlier research attempted to associate child abuse with one individual factor, their work has led them to operate from an ecological standpoint, because each predisposing factor is embedded within a whole network of features which have positive and negative effects on the situation. The ecological model of childrearing was proposed by Bronfenbrenner (1979), who argued that each child grows up within a series of interconnected systems (see Fig. 1). Each factor not only affects the child's way of life directly or indirectly, it also affects the other factors – for example, a family living on a pitifully low income cannot do anything to improve poor housing.

Although what some might call more 'scientific' methods of looking at and theorizing about human behaviour may have yielded useful and interesting data, the problem with them is that they take one or more aspects of human life and treat them as if they were being observed in a vacuum. With the ecological approach, life is not split into fragments, as Germain and Gitterman (1980: 5–6) comment:

> The ecological perspective provides an adaptive, evolutionary view of human beings in constant interchange with all elements of their environment. Human beings change their physical and social environments and are changed by them through processes of continuous reciprocal adaptation . . . Like all living systems, human beings must maintain a goodness-of-fit with the environment . . . adaptation is an active, dynamic and often creative process. Put another way, people, like all living

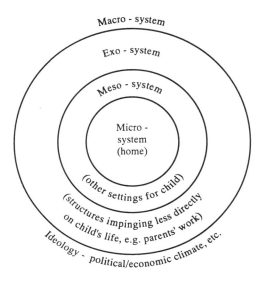

**Figure 1**  Bronfenbrenner's (1979) ecological model of human
development.

organisms, together with their environment, form an eco-
system in which each shapes the other.

Taking this perspective has implications for the whole of society,
not just for those working with abusing or neglectful parents, for
it may be that public policies related to the conditions in which
people are being forced to live, together with more explicit discussions about life with babies and children, including parenthood
education, are needed as strategies for preventing abuse and neglect.
Subcultural group factors may be misleading, because it is likely
that in some cases certain groups may be more sensitive to public
censure of the information they are about to divulge or otherwise.
Although Newson and Newson (1968: 450) suggest that 'Class I
and II mothers are on the whole less prepared to smack, and Class
V mothers are more inclined to do so', the evidence from their
research in the 1960s (gathered at a time when smacking was societ-
ally more acceptable) shows that in fact the Class V mothers in the
sample were most likely to disapprove of smacking in principle.
Of course, as the Newsons themselves point out, while it may be

possible to gain estimates of the frequency with which parents hit their children (according to their own testimony), the severity of the smacks is likely to vary from parent to parent and day to day.

Straus *et al.* (1980), presenting findings about the frequency of parental violence from a nationwide survey involving 1143 parents, argue that abuse of children is a widespread phenomenon in the USA, although a minority of incidents are reported. More than half the parents reported that they had hit or spanked their children during the past year, more than one in ten had hit their child with an object, over one in twenty had thrown something at a child and almost one in every two families contained a child who had been 'pushed, grabbed or shoved'. In a small number of cases, parents even admitted to having threatened a child with a gun or a knife. Researchers whose work has led them to the conclusion that abuse is the result of social stress and a poor ability to develop 'good' parenting skills, argue that what is needed are changes in (1) society's sanctioning of corporal punishment and (2) social isolation and lack of support.

Perhaps one of the most significant features which seems to emerge from inquiries into the deaths of young children who have died as a result of non-accidental injury, at least as far as early years teachers are concerned, is the fact that in many cases the parents had unreal expectations of their children. As Hamilton (1989: 34) states:

A great deal of child abuse seems to revolve around the activities of daily living with a child including crying, sleeping, feeding, toilet training, disciplining, dressing, playing, and grooming. When some children resist or show some stubbornness relative to these daily tasks, their behaviour is often interpreted as willful and defiant and may cause a parent to abuse out of frustration and anger, or to neglect because of feelings of helplessness.

Unless we build into our curriculum first-hand experience of what life with very young children is like, it is possible that there will not be enough time to change the attitudes and beliefs of those parents who may potentially maltreat their children. The time during pregnancy and imminent fatherhood, and perhaps even more so the lead up to step-fatherhood, are times which may be fraught with emotional turmoil and not best placed for the fostering of learning about human development.

Browne and Saqi's (1987) research at the University of Surrey has pointed to the fact that abusing parents often display inappropriate behaviour in response to their children's signals, and as a result the children involved may have behavioural difficulties which become manifest in the nursery or classroom. As far as the parents are concerned, this may result from a combination of causes: a knowledge and understanding of children's interests and behaviour patterns at different stages; the parents' own self-esteem and thus their belief in their child's liking for them; and their own experiences as children. When parents have been abused themselves as children, their own capacity for behaving more appropriately towards their children is likely to be affected by their experiences with adults other than their abusing parent(s). Additionally, when observed, abused children display a greater frequency of aggressive and destructive behaviour when compared with a 'non-abused' group of controls. Sometimes, the destructiveness is directed at themselves, as if confirming the poor self-image developed as a result of the displeasure they seem to give to their abusing parent(s). The situation is not irrevocable, thankfully, for retrospective studies of adults who were abused as children show that those who have experienced affection, support and encouragement – through a relationship in which they clearly 'mattered' to someone – are those survivors who are least likely to become abusers despite their early experiences (Lynch and Roberts 1982).

## Physical and emotional abuse in school

One of the places where children might find those 'persons to whom they matter' is in school. However, it may also be a place where many children experience physical abuse in the form of bullying. Ask any group of adults, including teachers and student teachers, if they can remember being bullied at school and most will remember quite vividly either being bullied or the strategies they adopted to avoid being bullied. During recent discussions, a group of Child Protection Co-ordinators from a number of local authorities recalled teachers by whom they had been taught, who had used both verbal and physical bullying techniques.

In a survey carried out in 1982 (Stephenson and Smith 1989), almost a quarter of the children in their final year in primary school were either bullies or victims, with boys forming 68 per cent of bullies and 63 per cent of victims – 65 per cent of the children who were both bullies and victims were boys. Boys are more likely to employ physical and verbal bullying, girls verbal bullying, teasing and isolation of the victim – forms of hurtful behaviour so well documented in the novel *Cat's Eye* by Margaret Attwood, about little girls growing up. Andy Slukin's (1981) research on playgrounds should have alerted us to the ways in which boys are pressurized into a form of masculinity which demands bravado, challenge and fights.

Stephenson and Smith (1989) found that schools with the lowest rates of bullying were those most likely to have a clear policy and belief that bullying should not be tolerated in school. Staff in such schools stressed the idea of the school as a 'family' or community, living together happily and where each member is cared for. Two out of three of the schools which reported no bullying were small and used cross-age groupings, which were thought to engender friendship and a less competitive ethos. One rather surprising outcome of this research was that physical punishment as a means of deterring bullying was supported by around half the teachers and a third of the school psychological service in the area studied. (Physical punishment was still allowed at this time.) Reid (1989) points out that bullies have often observed role models, (e.g. their fathers and male teachers) displaying powerfully aggressive behaviour, which suggests to them that they can get away with this behaviour if they are the biggest, strongest and most powerful.

Studies of bullying have indicated that it can begin in nursery school (Manning *et al.* 1978) and, if the aggressive behaviour is allowed to persist, the same children will be bullying at age seven or eight. Maccoby (1980) believes that children's cognitive development needs to be sufficiently advanced for them to understand that some of their actions hurt others. Judy Dunn (1987) found that mothers begin to talk about the feelings of others to their daughters at an earlier age than they do with their sons, and that this has an effect on their ability to empathize – so are we underestimating the age at which children can feel sympathy for others? Ann Lewis's (1990) research would suggest this is the case. A team undertaking research in nurseries, homes and schools (Manning *et al.* 1978) found that children who were bullies in group settings were not necessarily bullies at home. In this case it would be difficult for parents, perhaps, to accept the charges laid against their children when called in by teachers to discuss the matter. Searching for the possible causes of bullying, Manning and co-workers found that such children tended to come from over-controlling and dominating homes, and Mitchell (1973) suggests that where children observe levels of intra-family violence to such an extent that they regard it as normal family behaviour, it is hardly surprising that they are unable to interact with others without resorting to violence. Lefkowitz *et al.* (1977) link television violence with the learning of aggressive behaviour patterns, although Bandura's (1973) work suggests that this depends on whether or not the aggressive behaviour observed is rewarded or punished.

Jean La Fontaine's (1991) research on bullying resulted in the setting up of a new telephone helpline. The reason for this was that her research, unlike earlier studies where the researchers themselves defined what constituted bullying, actually sought the children's own definitions of bullying. Whereas adults had concentrated on violence, the children defined a wider range of behaviours and emphasized bullying as an act of rejection and hostility, often conveying 'a message' to the victims, that they are being outlawed. Again, this research brings to mind the way in which the narrator is treated in *Cat's Eye* (Attwood 1989).

**Research on strategies for preventing abuse in the home**

In surveying family violence over 300 years using archival evidence from the USA, Pleck (1987) suggests that although families may have become less hierarchical, they continue to be the site of violence for many women and children. What she advocates is a greater investment in alternatives (i.e. escape routes) for the maltreated, in the form of an expansion of childcare facilities, a reformed foster care system, and aid for women seeking separation and divorce. The problem is, she states, that any policies which appear to be an attack on 'family values' and the upholding of 'the family' are unlikely to attract political support and, as a result, scarce funding. Pleck (1987: 203) adds that, in her view, 'prevention' programmes are of 'dubious utility' because they fail to resolve the 'conflict between protecting the victim and preserving the family' (ibid: 202). Again we come back to the question of an overhaul of society, rather than our current 'tinkering'.

Holman (1988) evaluated the work of ten voluntary centres and, in his view, they engaged in activities aimed at: preventing children's reception into care or custody; preventing abuse and neglect; preventing children from experiencing poor parenting; and preventing severe social disadvantage. Holman argued that these types of centre were particularly effective because they were: part of voluntary organizations and thus were perceived as less threatening than statutory agencies; were open to all residents; were widely known within the community; achieved a high degree of local participation; and the staff were friendly and accepting, rather than 'professional', judgemental and distant.

Gibbons *et al.* (1990), suggest that we have very few rigorous research results to go on, and what there is is inconclusive about the effectiveness of any type of intervention so far tried in the field of child protection. They add, however, that reducing family poverty, developing advocacy and advice services, and developing procedures within social services to increase openness and accountability to clients would help. Furthermore, according to evidence from the USA (Berruetta-Clement *et al.* 1984), the provision of preschool education not only helps reduce the amount of time very young children spend in the home (for some a potential risk factor), but it has the potential for raising their levels of achievement and thus their self-esteem in adulthood – again, factors which appear to be implicated in abuse.

Research into seven family projects (Gibbons *et al.* 1990) offers some interesting insights which seem to build on those delineated by Holman. Gibbons and co-workers found that where staff held a 'service-giving' philosophy compared with a 'community development' philosophy, this affected role differentiation between staff. It also affected the balance in the activities occurring and the levels of involvement in management by local people. Funding appeared to be a difficult issue, since voluntary organizations were called to account and thus found it difficult to relinquish control to local residents. Further, when funding for a project was changed from some kind of grant arrangement to a statutory agency, there was often a shift to a more business-like approach, despite promises to retain the principle of partnership. Those projects which attempted to sustain themselves after funding ceased found it very difficult to do so, as did those where funds had initially been received from one type of agency (e.g. a children's charity), only for the emphasis to change – the needs of the elderly becoming the obvious focus for community action, as far as local residents were concerned. Other, possibly more positive aspects of these research findings included the success of the projects in attracting the involvement of disadvantaged families, whereas playgroups were attracting 'advantaged' families. The 'down' side of this feature of the family projects is that they could, therefore, have failed to involve families which might at times have needed support, but whose members shied away from involvement with what could have been perceived within the local community as signifying 'problem' families. Cochran (1986) in the USA and Pugh (1987) in the UK have both pointed out that schemes which are aimed at parental empowerment often fail if the parents subscribing to them are seen as failures or inadequate. Cochran's work involved all of the families in a neighbourhood and his research showed that this resulted in a lack of labelling, followed by greater success across the board in the development of the autonomous parent–child dyad (Bronfenbrenner's, 1979, term).

## Emotional abuse and neglect

Neglect as a form of abuse is one which has sometimes proved more difficult for professionals to deal with, because they may question their own value system and view of the world and wonder if they have the right to draw the attention of the authorities to families in which the children are always dirty, hungry, etc. Parents who neglect their children may do so for a number of reasons, some because of poverty and despair, some because they are drug or alcohol addicts. Between 1974 and 1983, the Registrar General of the UK reported the deaths of 184 children from hunger, exposure, thirst and neglect. This type of abuse is one which has itself been neglected by researchers, despite the fact that in 1986 the NSPCC reported that they suspected that as many as 200 'accidental' deaths of children were actually the result of inadequate supervision, i.e. neglect. Furthermore, the number of neglect cases is rising, with one in five under the age of one, and seven out of ten being under five (NSPCC 1989).

Emotional abuse is regarded as one factor which is common to all types of abuse. In fact, it may be that the damage inflicted during physical abuse and neglect will, in the long term, be emotional, rather than any lasting, visible signs on the body.

In 1986, the Royal College of Psychiatrists reiterated the points made by Mia Kellmer Pringle (1974) in her book *The Needs of Children*. The Royal College defined the needs as:

1 physical care and protection,
2 affection and approval,
3 stimulation and teaching,
4 discipline and control which are age-appropriate and consistent,
5 opportunity and encouragement to gradually acquire autonomy.

In the interests of mental health, Szur (1987: 112) adds 'appropriate physical contact; emotional support in times of stress and recognition as a separate individual'.

A study of 80 severely disadvantaged children by researchers at the Tavistock Clinic (Boston 1983) revealed that they generally had more difficulty forming and maintaining relationships than their more advantaged peers. Although the children had often found ways of dealing with the stress in their lives, and there were no set patterns to the stereotype of a 'deprived child', there were some common features, which included: a lack of trust; fear of suddenly being abandoned as worthless; sexualization; being unrewarding to those who worked with them, owing to a lack of pleasure in life. Some research has suggested that boys who have suffered emotional abuse will be aggressive and girls especially passive (e.g. Britton 1978), but others (e.g. Martin and Beezley 1977) have suggested that girls may be equally aggressive.

What this research tells us as teachers is that we have a role to play in acting as understanding and sympathetic adults in the lives of children who feel they are worthless, despite the fact that such children may actually prove extremely disruptive in the classroom. Sadly, schools have often responded to such behaviour, perhaps understandably, by being authoritarian and rejecting, the last things such a child needs.

# EIGHT

# RESEARCHING SEXUAL AND RITUALISTIC ABUSE

Sexual abuse did not begin to gain public recognition in any real sense until the late 1970s, and, as already stated, relatively little funding has been allocated to either research or training. Indeed, Jean La Fontaine (1990) suggests that some survivors who now work with sexually abused children feel that any research into the issue is a kind of 'academic voyeurism' (p. 17), but as her counter-argument goes, it is only by basing action on informed research that we can hope to be more effective in prevention and detection.

Teachers and their role have received particularly scant attention. Many colleagues who trained before and during the 1960s, 1970s and 1980s, relate the ways in which they look back over their careers and ponder the plight of children they probably 'missed' and thus failed, because the idea of anyone sexually abusing a child was thought to be (a) exceptional, (b) only likely to happen when a child came into contact with someone patently insane or (c) not a topic for inclusion in teacher training courses.

One would expect, however, that courses for teachers trained during the 1990s would have included at least some basic work on child abuse and protection. In a questionnaire survey I carried out in the autumn of 1990, tutors in 40 institutions offering early years courses were asked about the place of such training in their undergraduate and/or PGCE work. Twenty-one replied, all positively, some adding extra information, even kindly including examples of course outlines. It is difficult to say why the other 19 did not reply. One cannot be sure that this was because their replies would have been negative. However, a co-ordinator for a local authority asked new entrants to the profession to indicate if child abuse and protection had been covered in their initial training. She reported that of over 40 teachers (again the autumn of 1990), only seven had studied the issue as part of their course.

There may be many reasons for this, not least the recent pressure put on time by the National Curriculum and main subject study, which leaves little time to cover everything else, in what is becoming a 'portmanteau' course – more keeps being squeezed in but nothing much is thrown out. Child abuse may be a difficult issue for some trainers to tackle, especially when they need to have had time to come to terms with their own emotions first, and to feel confident that they could cope with any possible repercussions from students who may themselves have been subjected to abuse, as well as those who may be emotionally disturbed by the topic. Some argue that certain aspects of teaching require maturity, experience in a 'real teaching situation' before a person is ready to consider them. The problem with this approach is that students go out into the field even more unsure than they need to be, child abuse cases do not wait until the teacher concerned is 'ready', and sometimes student teachers, or new, young entrants to the profession, are the very people to whom children feel they can disclose about sexual abuse. Furthermore, although it is rare nowadays for teachers to have adopted the attitude that, once qualified, they need no updating in their training, it is dangerous to assume that training in such delicate work can be left totally to inservice sessions.

So why does child abuse pose such a problem for teacher training? First, there are historical reasons and reasons of time constraints. Secondly, some teacher trainers will have worked in the field a number of years ago, when child sexual abuse was not so commonly acknowledged. A final reason for this neglect in initial training may be the lack of reliable information from research, since this is needed to provide meaningful guidelines to young trainees. There are many forces in our society that are creating a situation in which it is difficult to imagine how we will increase our knowledge; for example, the response of the local MP, Stuart Bell (Bell 1988), in the Cleveland controversy was of the type to hinder the uncovering of new, reliable knowledge.

## Why has child sexual abuse only recently surfaced?

It may be that, in the past, the presence of members of the extended family could have acted as a protection against sexual abuse by older male relatives, rather like the protection against all forms of abuse revealed in Korbin's (1980, 1981) research into contemporary Chinese society. She has reported how neighbours will reprove parents, or, in severe cases, report them to the authorities. Certainly the role of the members of the extended family has been one of my own hypotheses for some time, though more recently a colleague suggested that this may be a naive assumption on my part. She argues that the general ignorance of many older female relatives, together with their relative powerlessness, could have been such that they failed to 'see' any abuse, in much the same way that society today often fails to do. This leads me to wonder if retrospective research into the incidence of abuse in families where the women are remembered as having been as my colleague describes, could be compared with that in families where, within the home at least, women were strong figures.

Whatever the women of the past may have been like, there are those who believe child sexual abuse did occur and was unacknowledged because of the power structures in society. We need to turn to the research evidence we do have to help us understand the issue and to formulate ideas about the role teachers can play in detection and prevention.

## What is the extent of the problem?

The problems which have already been discussed, relating to definitions and to the possibility of society's attitude to sexuality deterring disclosure even after the survivor reaches adulthood, create a number of anomalies in incidence data (Glaser and Frosh 1988). In 1986, David Finkelhor and associates reviewed research into the prevalence of child abuse in North America, some of it dating from the 1920s. Their clear presentation adds to our understanding of the research problems posed, since they arrange the work under headings according to the origins of the samples involved; they also give the number of subjects sampled. One group of projects studied volunteer samples, another college students, others were drawn from communities in certain areas, for example, Los Angeles in

1985. The sexual abuse ranged from 'serious sexual abuse in childhood, prior to age 16' to 'unwanted sexual acts before age 18, including exposure' (Finkelhor *et al.* 1986: 20). Prevalence, according to the different projects, ranged from 6 to 54 per cent for female survivors, and from 3 to 30 per cent for males.

Baker and Dunn (1985) attempted to explore the extent of child sexual abuse in the UK by interviewing a randomly selected group of men and women in their own homes, in a highly professional, confidential manner. Their survey revealed that child sexual abuse had been occurring in 10 per cent of the population, with a ratio of six girls to four boys. The abuse reported by these adults ranged from being subjected to 'erotic' language, to masturbation and sometimes full sexual intercourse. Table 1 shows that Baker and Dunn demonstrated the discrepancy between the real incidence of abuse, especially when boys are the victims, and that reported to the police.

**Table 1** Results of the survey of patterns of sexual abuse by Baker and Dunn (1985)

|  | Males (%) | Females (%) |
|---|---|---|
| Intrafamilial | 13 | 14 |
| Extrafamilial | 44 | 30 |
| Stranger | 43 | 56 |
| One-off incident | 59 | 66 |
| Repeated (same person) | 30 | 18 |
| Multiple abusers | 11 | 16 |
| No contact | 48 | 55 |
| Contact | 49 | 40 |
| Intercourse | 5 | 5 |

While this study appears to have been conducted in an exemplary manner, Jean La Fontaine (1990) raises several of the issues discussed in Chapter 5 concerning the integrity of researchers and the need for those whose experiences they wish to investigate to trust them. She argues that this alone can affect the numbers of reported cases, and compared a rate of 3 per cent uncovered by a BBC national survey, whereas a very rigorous study, conducted by trusted and meticulous researchers in Cambridge, apparently found a rate of 48 per cent. La Fontaine goes on to discuss the fact that the definition of abuse used was 'very wide' and that no differentiation was possible between those cases in which the abuse involved contact and those in which it did not. Furthermore, this study did not address the sexual abuse of boys. Somehow, this seems to negate the claim that this was 'the most careful attempt of its time to provide information on undisclosed cases of sexual abuse' (La Fontaine 1990: 63). Certainly, the study was important in that its findings 'made it very clear that far more cases [of sexual abuse] are kept hidden than are revealed' (ibid.).

La Fontaine also makes the crucial point that researchers may be making unjustified assumptions about the prevalence of child sexual abuse as occurring randomly in the population as a whole. Children whose parents were abused, children whose siblings have been/are being abused, and children living in an area where there are abusers, may be more likely to experience abuse than children not subject to these conditions. Additionally, some children may appear more than once in certain forms of sampling. Thus, incidence rates will be affected by sampling techniques. La Fontaine suggests that research in this country is in its infancy, and qualitative data, together with extensive quantitative research findings from a variety of disciplines, needs to be carried out. While a minimum prevalence rate of 10 per cent has been suggested, La Fontaine (1990: 67) believes that rates will always be underestimated, because 'some secrets will always be kept'.

## Who are the victims?

Because of the tremendous courage it takes to cope with abuse and its consequences, and because 'victim' is a word which implies passivity, many working in the field prefer to use the term 'survivor'. Certainly, it better indicates the struggle made, the fight to go on living, and the attempt to make sense of what a person in a position of power, and possibly loved in spite of the abuse, could do to one. While those who excuse paedophiles argue that children should be entitled to whatever activity they agree to in a loving, close relationship, their argument has to be destroyed by the counter-evidence that children do not usually understand sexual activity, they therefore cannot give consent and that often children are trapped in a situation in which they dare not refuse or complain, even where their compliance is not the result of physical force or threats of violence. (For survivors' testimony see Angelou 1984; Spring 1987; Rouf 1991.)

### What we think we know about signs and symptoms

The most important point to remember about the signs and symptoms of any form of abuse is that one must treat them with caution, and ensure that other evidence, perhaps something the child says, corroborates the 'evidence'. Even if more than one sign is present, there may be another explanation for the child's condition.

The kinds of physical symptoms which might indicate sexual abuse include chronic itching or pain in the genitals, vaginal discharge, a sore bottom, tummy ache, bedwetting, nightmares and eating disorders. If children become aggressive or suddenly have tantrums, or the reverse, become overly compliant, insecure, isolate themselves from friends, suddenly do not perform as well at school, or indulge in too frequent washing or bathing, seem to lose trust in a familiar adult, or avoid him, or attempt to inflict wounds on themselves, then these too may be signs of abuse. Sometimes workers have noted that children will start to use sexually explicit behaviours in their play, or talk about sexual matters inappropriate to their age, or they may approach adults in a sexually overt manner, or masturbate overtly and frequently.

### Why children do not tell

Staff who have observed some of the above signs and become alerted to the possibility of sexual abuse may wonder why children are not disclosing to them. Anne Peake (1989b) suggests that the main reasons why young children do not do so are: (1) young children do not have the language to express what is happening to them; (2) they do not have 'permission' (and they have generally been taught to obey older people), and it is likely that the perpetrator has made real or implied threats to prevent their telling; and (3) children may not understand that they have been duped into being abused, i.e. they may mistake the perpetrator's behaviour for part of a 'normal', affectionate relationship.

## Referral rates by teachers

Between 1983 and 1987, the percentage of cases of suspected abuse (overall) reported by teachers fell from about 15 to 8 per cent of all referrals to the NSPCC (NSPCC 1989), yet the rate of detection of sexual abuse cases increased from 0.08 to 0.65 children per thousand. Furthermore, the NSPCC (1989: 48) point out that in their view sexual abuse 'is attracting the attention and developing skills of staff', and a warning note is sounded that workers should not, as a result, overlook the 'softer' categories of abuse. It has to be said, however, that sexual abuse referrals comprised the second largest category of cases reported by schools and 'pre-schools', according to these NSPCC statistics. One of the features of recent statistics which may cause even greater distress to all concerned is the numbers of referrals of very young children in this category, sexual abuse having previously been assumed to be perpetrated against teenage girls – the 'Lolita factor'.

A further finding concerning perpetrators is their likelihood of being stepfathers (rather than short-term cohabitants), and that they are also likely to have been in a relationship with the mother and the child for longer than carers of children in other categories (NSPCC 1989). In other words, the cause of sexual abuse cannot be laid at the door of unstable or short-term adult relationships. 'It is the quality more than the duration of the relationship that is important' (NSPCC 1989: 48). A non-parent was implicated in almost a third of sexual abuse cases, and children sexually abused during access visits to non-custodial parents figured increasingly in the statistics.

Emphasis on stepfathers (wicked stepfathers?) and other relatives can be dangerous because it deflects attention away from the statistics which reveal the extent of abuse by 'natural' fathers of their own children. As stated above, some of the children abused during access visits have been visiting their 'natural' fathers. In other cases, fathers have taken advantage of their own daughters and prevented them from telling their mothers by using threats or other machinations (e.g. see Rouf 1991).

## Women as perpetrators

According to available statistics, perpetrators of sexual abuse are overwhelmingly male. Cases reported to the NSPCC between 1983 and 1987 indicated that while the natural father was the suspected perpetrator in 32 per cent of cases, and a stepfather in 15 per cent, a lone mother was suspected in 2 per cent and a mother colluding with her partner in a further 2 per cent of cases. Further, while most men and boys who do report having been sexually abused have suffered at the hands of older men, some people argue that abuse of males by females is masked because of our prevalent ideology. They argue that males who have been sexually abused by women are unlikely to report it because the act will not be perceived as abuse; rather, 'seduction' by an older woman is seen as a positive experience in a macho culture, despite the fact that for some boys this may not accord with how they felt about the incident. Further, women are generally regarded as being sexually passive, so that the whole concept of such abuse could be unthinkable. However, as Emily Driver (1989) suggests, we should be open-minded about the possible extent of abuse by females, and recognize the potentially damaging effects. It does seem unlikely, however, that such acts by women are common. There is scant evidence of women's hidden crimes of flashing, molestation and rape, and it seems reasonable to assume that rape by an adult male who is stronger and who effects penetration, will be a greater violation than most forms of sexual abuse where the perpetrator is a woman. Naturally, there are exceptions, such as the cases where Myra Hindley colluded with Moors Murderer Ian Brady. Lynne Segal (1989) argues that the gendered nature of rape, sadistic pornography and violence does not actually explain them; she sees the problem in terms of the way societies construct masculinity, and in the general levels of violence in those societies. Additionally, we may be selective in the way in which we interpret the same behaviour by parents of different sexes, for example, a parent sharing a bed with an older child in a society in which this is not considered 'normal'.

## Long-term effects

The later adjustment of children who have been sexually abused may be difficult owing to a range of factors. According to Hall and Lloyd (1989), these include traumatic sexualization (e.g. confusing sexual activity with love), betrayal, powerlessness, stigma and enforced silence. The long-term consequences may include low self-esteem, confusion (e.g. a general fear of men), emotional

reactions and anxiety problems, depression, isolation and interpersonal difficulties, physical complaints, negative reactions to
medical or hospital treatment, sleep disturbance, eating disorders,
'victim' behaviour, and problems with trust.

### Research on treatment for survivors and perpetrators

Drawing on her research to convey the potential long-term effects
of abuse, Jean La Fontaine (1990: 212–13) states that even if

> . . . the relationship is gentle and affectionate, a sexually
> abused child may suffer serious harm . . . Serious psycho-
> logical damage may be caused by a child's love for the abuser
> and the resulting conflict of emotions.

Many experienced workers will tell you that each case of child
abuse is unique, for each child and the setting in which the abuse
occurs, together with the perpetrator and his or her relationship
with the child, are the characteristics producing that unique event,
or set of events (Furniss 1987). Although the most immediate need
is for the abuse to be stopped, long-term there is a need for therapy,
since many victims do ultimately attempt suicide or turn to drugs
and drink. Many may abuse, in their turn, or be incapable of forming meaningful relationships, especially where they may turn into
adult sexual relationships.

La Fontaine (1990) challenges the view that it may not always
be the abuse itself which causes a child psychological harm, but the
effects of the shocked reactions of the rest of society. Most adults
who have kept their childhood abuse a secret will, when they do
speak out, state that they did not like what was happening to them,
yet it may not have been until adulthood that they became aware
that they were wronged in the eyes of society, and that they were
in no way to blame. Further, disclosing abuse may be deeply distressing to children and, indeed, to adults years after the abuse has
ceased (Miller 1980).

### Research on teachers and their feelings about their role in protecting children from sexual abuse

Corinne Wattam's (1990) study for the NSPCC of teachers' experiences with children who have or who may have been sexually abused

indicates changes in behaviour or personality were key indicators for teachers, the initial alerting factors which then caused them to seek further confirmation. The teachers in the survey knew of the procedures and knew they should report suspicions to the Named Person in the school, but since much of the more general information gathered by the teachers which might indicate abuse was perceived by them as ambiguous, they questioned either the information itself or their obligation to act immediately. One of the factors causing a dilemma to the teachers who volunteered for the survey was confidentiality. The second area of difficulty lay in decisions about bringing sexual abuse into the curriculum.

Wattam concluded that the teachers in her survey believed that child protection was a part of their role, but that not all teachers may be quite so committed, because many cases of abuse go unrecognized. A very substantial proportion of the respondents in her survey had no experience of working with children who had been sexually abused, 330 out of 385 stating that to their knowledge they had not come into contact with any abused children. Since an estimated 10 per cent of the population may be subjected to some form of such abuse, it may be, as one of Wattam's respondents suggested, that the teachers have not been sufficiently trained to recognize an abused child. Wattam identified three impediments to reporting, even if some training in identification has been undertaken: (1) a refusal to believe that abuse really happens; (2) sexual abuse is a particularly difficult type of abuse for teachers to deal with in a society which is permeated with restrictions and taboos about discussing sex or private and confidential matters openly; (3) the difficulty of accepting that short-term damage caused by referral may actually be less traumatic in the long run, compared with the effects of sexual abuse of a child by an adult.

## Research on ritualistic abuse – to believe or not to believe, that is the question

Jean La Fontaine is currently researching evidence for ritualistic abuse for the Department of Health. It may be that data for this research will prove the most elusive ever. The whole subject brings together not only the secrecy of the sexual abuse of children, but illegal and forbidden practices involving ritual sacrifice, dead babies

– with questions about where these would have come from – and power over the minds of initiates.

It would appear that the incidence of satanic abuse as part of the practices of a religious group is very low. Beatrix Campbell (1990), however, argues that we deny satanism because we do not want to think it exists, but in so doing we deny the claims of children, and adults, who have come forward and reported this. She suggests that the way in which their testimony was rejected, dismissed as fantasies, is reminiscent of Freud's denial of sexual abuse in his women patients. John Cornwell (1991) spent a year investigating claims and counter-claims for his book *Powers of Darkness, Powers of Light*, and although he reports that evidence is hard to come by, he argues that the imagination can be very powerful. What we need to ask, therefore, is: (1) might the 'satanic' rituals used by a group be cover for collective child sexual abuse, and (2) might more widely defined forms of ritualistic/religious abuse be more common in society, and therefore require our considered attention?

Many injustices have been enacted upon children in the name of religion, often 'for their own good'. Religious leaders could be among those helping to eradicate such abuse, and many indeed are offering support where it is needed (Armstrong 1991). For some vulnerable members of society, religious communities offer warmth and acceptance, but such individuals are also easily manipulated.

With any credo, where new members, especially the young, are expected to accept unquestioningly the tenets of that religion, there is the possibility of a misuse of power. Roman Catholic and Jewish friends have told me of physical punishments they endured during classes intended to instil faith, and some Muslim children have reported to me the physical punishments they are threatened with for not learning to recite the Koran as required. Other, more subtle 'punishments' have been employed, such as being excluded from community gatherings and being 'sent to Coventry' for questioning teachings in some of the other established religious groups, and these strategies serve to instil conformity. In other words, most religions demand unswerving devotion and obedience to God and to the faith, and in the majority of cases they uphold, above everything else, the supremacy of those vested with the power of God – usually adult males. Furthermore, when cases are brought to light, as in the recent treatment of a Jewish family who alerted the police about abuse of their children (*The Guardian* 28 August 1991), vulnerable groups close ranks because they fear the publicity will give excuses to those who wish to eradicate their group or persecute them. In this case, therefore, there was a reinforcing of the patriarchal tenets of the group and ostracism of the family of the abused children, instead of openly acknowledged action to eradicate the abuse.

Whether or not we believe that witchcraft and devil worship are on the increase, or whether some groups are using young people's fears about the devil and his power, induced through the very religions others (the good) support, really is immaterial – it is the fact that children are being unscrupulously manipulated that matters. In fact, the belief system employed may not even be religious, as the example of the trial of the Leicestershire social worker who abused children and young colleagues in residential homes testifies. One social work recruit reported at the trial that he believed allowing himself to be buggered by the defendant would 'make him into a better social worker' (*The Guardian* 14 October 1991).

The final absurdity for me, in relation to reports of satanism, was the publishing of a list of objects which should not be permitted in schools because of their supposed 'devil-worship' connections – the list included Indian rugs. Yoga classes were also banned from some church halls. Surely we should be sceptical of this type of propaganda, as it smacks rather of power politics – if you smear the opposition long enough, people will begin to believe the smears. If there is real concern about what is happening to children, then the misuse of religious power and beliefs, no matter what those beliefs, should be examined and religious teaching discussed to see how it may be contributing to (a) the propounding of unquestioning belief systems by adults and older teenagers and the exploitation of children through the use of those beliefs to frighten them; (b) the ways in which a religion and the structures of its establishment undermine women and uphold the power of men who are the main perpetrators of this kind of abuse; (c) the ways in which a religion induces a total acceptance in children of obedience to those older and with more 'clout' than themselves.

## • PART TWO •

# IDENTIFYING AND HELPING ABUSED CHILDREN

# NINE

# IT DOESN'T HAPPEN HERE: SCHOOLS AND CHILD PROTECTION

During the late 1980s and early 1990s, the arrangements for the implementation of the National Curriculum and the assessment of children, including SATs (Standard Assessment Tasks, or, as government representatives insist, the 'tests' for seven-year-olds), have rumbled on in the UK, leaving English and Welsh primary school teachers feeling rather like those who rode in the tumbrils of Paris 200 years ago. Meanwhile, the issue of child abuse has exploded in the media a number of times, shattering children, families and local authority social services departments.

In the main, teachers have remained out of the spotlight as these desperately sad events have unfolded. In one recent case, where a toddler was beaten to death, the involvement of anyone from the teaching profession would have been highly unlikely, since we in Britain do not yet train teachers to work with this age group, despite the fact that other EC partners see wisdom in such a development. In other well-publicized cases involving traumatic sexual abuse allegations, teachers would indeed have been in contact with the children taken into care, because of their ages. Yet it has been rare for teachers to be given more than a passing reference, if any.

No doubt the local education authorities of the areas in question heaved a sigh of relief at avoiding such publicity, especially when one examines earlier reports where teachers are mentioned, such as that concerning Jasmine Beckford (Brent Panel of Inquiry

1985), but there is a worrying side to all this too. Most documents about child abuse and protection, ranging from the Report of the Cleveland Inquiry (Butler-Sloss 1988) to the report of a seminar held in Scotland in 1987 (Stone 1989), appear to have had little or no input from classroom teachers or even heads of schools.

Why should this be? Do teachers simply not 'see' abuse when it occurs, nor regard children's welfare as part of their responsibilities? Are teachers being left out by the 'crisis professionals', i.e. the social workers, police and doctors? Are teachers simply too busy at present with the National Curriculum and all else that the 1988 Education Reform Act has thrust upon them, to cope with the apparently growing need for child protection?

## Role definition

There has always been some disagreement, even among teachers themselves, about whether they should become involved in the more pastoral aspects of work with children. Some will argue that teachers are meant to confine themselves to teaching – or, under the more current view, to children's learning of skills and knowledge, and the development of concepts and attitudes to that learning. The countering group will add, 'All this and more, for children cannot and will not learn if they are troubled.' Further, this latter group will probably perceive their role to include that of adult ally, protector and advocate. Certainly, as far as early years teachers are concerned, they are frequently seen by their pupils as someone who cares about them, someone they can trust, and a child's teacher may well be the adult closest to that child, outside the family.

Following the Cleveland Report (Butler-Sloss 1988), guidelines were issued by the DES instructing each school to appoint a senior member of staff as their named contact, who should deal with any cases of suspected abuse to children in the school, cooperate with outside agencies, and be both the delegate attending training courses and provider of in-house training for staff. By the summer of 1990, Alan Howarth, one of the education ministers, reported that he was pleased with the progress schools had made in carrying out these requirements (DES 1990). While Alan Howarth proclaimed this progress, I was still hearing a plethora of anecdotal evidence of schools in which no-one knew if they had a nominated person, or, if they had, the staff were ignorant of who this was. In one school, a young teacher colleague who volunteered to go on a course and to act as the named contact was refused permission because of National Curriculum work. This was at a school where even the head did not know who the nominated person was, since he did not know he should have appointed someone. Several teachers reported to me that the majority of the staff in the schools where they worked still maintained that child abuse 'didn't happen in this area', and, as a result, any attempts to encourage whole-school training had met with opposition and closed minds.

The fact that child protection is often placed in the hands of local education welfare officers may seem appropriate in one sense, because of their social work expertise, yet it is important to ask whether such a strategy appears to absolve teachers themselves of having any significant responsibility. On the other hand, this may be a positive move if handled correctly, for it emphasizes the collaborative nature of the exercise. On the negative side, EWOs have not, usually, had classroom teaching experience, so their understanding of the difficulties teachers face may be limited.

Certainly, one feels that the sheer volume of content imposed on teachers via the National Curriculum Programmes of Study implies that 'the teacher's role is to teach' would be the official view of the current government, since there is little time to cover this and carry out continuous assessment procedures about children's learning of this content, let alone form close relationships with children, observe their free activity, make notes of anything disturbing, work with parents, follow child abuse guidelines *and* undertake the training needed to understand the whole issue of child protection. There have already been reports of the relationships between pupils and teachers in primary schools being damaged by the requirements of the National Curriculum – teachers have commented on deteriorating behaviour in the schools piloting the SATs, and parents have noted that their children feel they are being watched constantly by teachers for recording purposes (e.g. Hughes *et al.* 1991; NUT 1991).

As with other legislation I will discuss later, one has the impression that the government is asking teachers to comply with regulations which actually conflict. Is it any wonder, then, that the 1988 Education Reform Act, which affects all children rather than an almost invisible few, enshrined in law, and with funded materials and training, has taken precedence? Additionally, it is difficult to imagine where teachers would find the time for child protection training. Teachers of Key Stage 1 (teaching pupils aged 5–7, the first to be tested on the National Curriculum) are already spending inordinate amounts of time on their work (some working a 70-hour week; Campbell and Neill 1990).

### Failure to 'see' abuse

Schools fell from initiating 15% of the registrations in 1983 to 8% in 1987 . . . The main decrease was in the physically injured children. 17% of these registrations were initiated by schools and preschools in 1983 falling to 13% in 1987 . . . It might be expected that, with the increasing number of registrations each year, and in particular of school aged children, the schools would have increased their contribution to the initiating process. (NSPCC 1989: 35)

While the press pillory social workers for acting either too hastily (as in the cases of Cleveland, Nottingham and Orkney), or too slowly, as in the recent physical abuse case resulting in the death of a toddler, teachers tread softly. Yet while they may not have the same overall responsibility as social workers, they are still obliged to report suspected abuse. For teachers and youth workers involved in day-to-day interactions with teenagers, this can sometimes be a fearful responsibility, since children of this age – and they are still defined as children in law until they are 18 – may expect confidences to be treated as such. For primary school teachers, especially those who work with the youngest children, confidentiality is unlikely to figure in this sense, unless it is the parent who comes to ask for help in overcoming a problem connected with the abuse of a child.

Teachers are likely to be wary of rushing into any action because they have close relationships with many of their pupils' parents during this phase of education. They do see their role as one of supporting families. Ill-informed, damaging action would not only harm the very children and families they seek to nurture, it would probably destroy years of work building up home–school links with an entire community.

Additionally, teachers of young children are thought to believe in childhood innocence (King 1978). Perhaps this in itself acts as one impediment to their acceptance of child sexual abuse. However, many teachers who have worked with young children for years are experienced enough to distinguish between displays of childhood sexuality which they recognize as part of a 'normal' child's exploration of everything around them, and the disturbing evidence of abuse.

If they perceive themselves as 'protectors and allies' of young children, then teachers are unlikely to be supportive of what has happened recently in the UK, for in some local authorities children were removed from their homes – and as a result their schools too – and placed with total strangers. Though this type of action is intended to protect those children suspected of being subjected to criminal acts, many teachers, aware of the importance of continuity, must question the wisdom of the damage and pain inflicted on the children by such a 'police raid' approach. After all, it is as if the children themselves are the criminals. Additionally, there will be variations in the extent to which follow-up procedures allow for a familiar teacher to remain with the child during an investigation. Most teachers are likely to feel distressed at the idea of encouraging children to avoid 'stranger danger' and then packing them off with people they have never set eyes on before. The feeling that to act may not be in the child's best interests can become overwhelming, yet, until one acts, how can one assess exactly what is in the best interests of the child? Presumably, certain important aspects of the story cannot come to light without an investigation.

## The need for training

The fact that only a small proportion of teachers have received any training is also likely to have exacerbated the profession's feelings of vulnerability. There is so much that is still unknown, especially where sexual abuse is concerned. It is understandable that those teachers who feel they are not competent, due to a lack of training and experience, fail to act. Even experienced teachers often lack confidence, despite local authority guidelines, since they report that these often simply complicate matters. Though the guidelines give the impression that the procedures are straightforward and easy to follow, and there are those in positions of power within local education authorities for whom teacher action is a clear-cut affair, there are many at the grass-roots level who believe that each individual case raises many questions and the whole field is filled with uncertainty.

Some schools have attempted to incorporate proactive work with children into their curriculum, but have not first taken the time (and a year seems the very least one must take for such staff development for it to be successful) to ensure that their staff could cope. All these factors have hindered teachers identifying abuse.

### A more positive future?

In October 1991, the Children Act 1989 came into force, and with it, new approaches to the needs of children. Underpinning this Act are four main principles: the child's interests as paramount, including ensuring that the child's views are heard; parental responsibility (rather than rights) and support for families from local authorities, aimed at the prevention of family break-up; recognition of the child's racial, cultural, linguistic and religious background; cooperation and collaboration among workers in the voluntary and maintained services.

As a result of this Act, it will become less likely that children are removed from the care of their parents, unless the child's life is threatened. Thus, only in cases of serious, imminent danger would police and social workers 'rush in'. However, there is some scepticism in the field that it will still, generally speaking, be children rather than the person or persons suspected of abuse who are removed from the family home.

Two planks of the 1988 Education Reform Act – the local financial management of schools (LMS) and opting out (becoming an independent school) – could, however, constrain the types of support and inservice training available for teachers, thus affecting their ability to act appropriately within the new legal framework of the Children Act 1989. First, National Curriculum demands leave little time for anything else and, secondly, competition between schools for pupils could mean that some shy away from any developments which may be misinterpreted by parents (e.g. INSET on drugs, or child abuse and protection). On the 'plus' side, however, the clauses of the Children Act 1989 requiring support from local authorities for children in need, which would include children suspected of being at risk of some form of abuse, could be used to demand that better funding be made available to undertake this work.

Much physical and emotional abuse and neglect is thought to be the result of parental stress, bad housing, poverty and a lack of knowledge about young children. Sexual abuse, too, may develop from feelings of self-hatred (often the result of having been sexually abused as a child), a need to derive a sense of power by abusing one's position and strength, and lack of recognition for the victim's personhood. Could we, as a society, both protect the young from all these forms of violation and prevent adults from becoming perpetrators by changing societal structures and by developing better supportive networks which could well be centred on schools? The Children Act 1989 gives teachers the opportunity as well as the legal backing to call for their inclusion in the collaborative work which will be vital. If such work is recognized as part of the teacher's role, and if schools wish to develop their partnerships with parents – one of the principles of the 1988 Education Reform Act – that collaborative support should surely include work to prevent abuse in the community.

Teachers are in daily contact with many children, most of them hopefully not the victims or survivors of abuse. The majority of early childhood educators have been trained in child development, although this unfortunately appears to be regarded as unimportant by some (Alexander *et al.* 1992) in the current debate about education. If they are early years teachers, they are also likely to be in daily contact with adult members of the family. In contrast, most of the personnel from the other services are more frequently in contact with families in difficulties of one kind or another. It seems possible that teachers are those most experienced in the whole range of child behaviours. This surely should be a reason for giving them a more central role in child protection work than they have had to date.

In order to achieve this, as a short-term measure, every member of the teaching profession will need to become informed, to acknowledge their own emotions, to develop the context for listening to children, to be able to keep objective, confidential records, to support parents and work collaboratively with colleagues from fields other than education. Both whole-school, area and inter-professional training will be needed. Supportive networks for teachers themselves will need to be set up. In the long term, teachers may wish to work as advocates for the structural changes in society which would aim to eradicate child abuse.

The unprecedented and progressive rhetoric of the Children Act 1989 can only become a reality if all workers, including school teachers, are granted the resources, training and time needed to undertake and fulfil the important aspirations it enshrines. In the following chapters, some of the strategies for providing positive support to children, families, teachers and their colleagues in school and outside it are explored.

# TEN

# THE LISTENING SCHOOL: ACKNOWLEDGING AND SUPPORTING ABUSED CHILDREN

During the last ten years there has been a positive development in primary education in which the view of a classroom as one teacher's own private domain has been challenged. Not only has there been greater encouragement for colleagues to collaborate in planning coherent and progressive interpretations of the curriculum, in order to make sense to children as they move through the system, there has been a growth of interest in what whole-school development entails – from innovation and curriculum leader roles, to evaluation including discussion of to whom exactly whole-school policies apply. In part this has been the result of increased accountability, in part a realization that the curriculum has become so broad and so complex that generalists are thought to need the support of specialists (DES 1978).

The way in which schools go about the task of whole-school development will depend on many factors, including encouragement from both within and without, the existing ethos of the school, and whether teaching staff are open to the idea of such development.

Andrew Pollard and Sarah Tann (1987) have explored the ethos, or 'feel', of a school, suggesting that 'perspectives, behaviour and action in schools are very often influenced by established conventions, expectations and norms' (p. 176). They argue that these norms often remain implicit, unspoken and that they are subject to the influence of certain individuals within the school population, according to the status, power, charisma and authority of that person. Thus, according to their analysis, a headteacher is likely to have considerable influence on the school's development, while another person may feel marginal in this respect. Pollard and Tann suggest that assemblies are a good place in which to observe heads' aims, through their approaches to the symbolic and ritual functions, as well as through the way management issues are handled at this time. Additionally, others, such as the deputy head, postholders, caretaker, secretary, parents, governors and, of course, children themselves, contribute to the institutional atmosphere of the school.

During a process of self-evaluation, or the formulation of a School Development Plan, staff may decide they need to formulate a policy statement about some aspect of practice. This could be specifically tied to areas of the curriculum, or it could be a policy which permeates the school's life and work, such as equal opportunities, parental involvement or special educational needs. The policy would then have implications for practice, either as a reaffirmation of existing practice which has been overtly recognized and agreed, or as a statement of intent, which would need to be monitored and supported to ensure policy did indeed become practice and evaluated for possible improvements – whether that be at the policy or practice level, or both.

In their book *The Self-evaluating Institution*, Clem Adelman and Robin Alexander (1982) remind us that school reviews are 'political' affairs, since they will always entail judgements made according to a particular value base, and thus a rejection of some other values. These judgements may mean that some personnel within the school are being overridden, and the result may even be a redistribution of power within that school. For example, in a school where the staff have consistently rejected the notion that parents in their area could abuse their children, the headteacher's encouragement of a member of staff in promoting the idea of a school policy on protection, and the development of training, may be met with dismay and lack of self-confidence, despite apparent acquiescence.

We might begin by convincing colleagues that the evidence we have, and the statistics to hand at present, indicate that there is a need for us all to be concerned: first, because we know from adults who kept their childhood suffering secret that this is something which occurs in all socio-economic groups and, secondly, because children who are being abused are likely to be unable to achieve their learning potential, owing to the psychological and physical effects of abuse. There are exceptions, such as Khadj Rouf (1990), who writes of her own experience of sexual abuse by her father, beginning around the age of five, and of how she later realized she could become pregnant, but how

> School was the only escape that I had now. I worked really hard and was in the top sets for most subjects. I was the model pupil. Compliant, attentive, quiet. I was painfully shy. Nobody thought my behaviour strange because my behaviour was completely acceptable. I was a good girl. (Rouf 1991: 7)

In a school where children are seen and not heard, the barriers erected as a result of reluctance to address the question 'Are we a listening school?' may seem insuperable, not least because the first step, recognition of a child's right to be heard, demands such an enormous step in attitudinal change.

Pollard and Tann (1987) suggest that there are stages which one might consider adopting as strategies for whole-school development and, in the following, I have based child protection policy development on these.

First, staff need to be persuaded that innovation is necessary. In the case of child protection policies, this means convincing colleagues that the current ethos of the school might need adaptation if teachers are to fulfil their statutory duties to detect and report abuse, and that it is in the interests of our future society that preventative work should be part of the teacher's role. Following this, especially with such a sensitive issue, there would need to be a period of learning, possibly involving the support of other colleagues from the local authority – the child protection co-ordinator, education welfare officers, educational psychologists, and so on. Once the team has a deeper understanding of the issue, and has had a chance to explore their own attitudes and values concerning abuse and its possible causes, a re-evaluation of the school's current practices would be necessary, in order to pinpoint factors within the school which may constrain or facilitate change. Following this, ideas to ensure the provision of a supportive atmosphere in the school will be important, and will lead to collective decisions about a plan of action.

Some of the questions teachers might ask themselves concerning the development of a listening ethos would include:

- Which of the following groups have a voice in decision making about factors affecting their lives:

| | |
|---|---|
| caretaker | children |
| cleaning staff | class teachers |
| classroom ancillary staff | community leaders, e.g. clergy |
| deputy headteacher | governors |
| headteacher | meals staff |
| parents | secretary |

Go through the list again and assess the relative importance (or otherwise) of the decisions these people may make, or are allowed to make. Pugh and De'Ath (1989) demonstrate the ways in which powerful groups within a school may believe they are sharing decisions, while they are really only allowing those without commensurate power to be involved in very limited decisions.

Consider the following:

- How is the school organized and how are the classrooms organized? Are there areas which afford privacy and enable disclosure, or encourage parents to feel conversations will be confidential?
- What are the rules relating to playtimes, etc.? Are children made to go outside (weather permitting)? This could be a time when a child might seek a quiet conversation with a member of staff.
- Are teachers approachable? Do they talk about children, or their parents, in front of others? Is the school welcoming? Would 'new' (or even 'old') parents find their way around easily?
- Are teachers always rushing about, appearing to have no time for intimate conversations?
- How much do we really know about the interests of individual children? Are there some children about whom we know nothing, other than their names, addresses, appearance, record so far, work – as made manifest by products, rather than our observations of how they go about an activity?
- Having gone through these points, evaluate the evidence for the responses made and ask yourself why questions, e.g. Why is a particular child the one you know little about? Why are some teachers approachable?

If, initially, it has been decided to carry out the above evaluation and take steps to ensure the school is a 'listening institution', how will the staff cope if children do start to disclose to them about abuse they have suffered? What kinds of preparation are all the teaching staff likely to need? In the first place, they too will want to be listened to, so while the school is being evaluated for its ethos relating to children and parents, it should also examine the following questions:

- Do staff offer a supportive network to each other? Is the head accessible, open and approachable?
- How is the team organized? Who is the Named Person, i.e. who is the senior teacher with responsibility for liaising with other agencies, and for ensuring the school's child protection role is understood by all staff? Where are the Local Authority Child Protection Guidelines? Do we know what they contain?
- If there is already a policy statement and a Named Person, is the system working?

Sometimes teachers have found their senior colleagues unable to accept their fears about a child, and in the end, the distraught, individual teacher has been forced to take the case anonymously to the NSPCC or the local social services, and this is something they have a right to do as citizens, although most no doubt wish they had not been left feeling isolated and unsupported in their decision.

If teachers are to be open to the possibility of disclosures, not only does their approachability, their classroom environment and accessibility matter, but their reactions will be crucial. In schools where the decision has been made to implement whole-school training, one of the most important aspects of that training will involve confronting one's own emotions. Teachers will need to be able to listen with sympathy, reassurance, and without betraying shock or distaste or any other emotion which children might interpret as meaning finding them at fault.

## Confronting our emotions

As we grow up in our own families, within our own communities, our feelings about a whole range of issues become embedded in the accepted rituals of our daily lives, or are excluded from our consciousness because they are taboo. Unless we are able to raise to our consciousness, think about, talk about and confront issues about which we feel strong emotions, we are simply hiding from them by burying them deep within ourselves. In certain situations, these feelings may come, involuntarily, to the surface, and it is then that we have problems. For example, Herbert (1990) recently undertook some research into the circumstances surrounding the birth of babies with Down's Syndrome. She found that although she had not specifically asked to see the mothers alone, the fathers opted out of the evening interviews. Many of the mothers told of how they had never before talked through their distressing experiences – first in hospital when told of their child's condition and then later in the outside world when faced by the embarrassed reactions of family and friends. Despite the fact that they, as a group, had grown to love their children just as they had their other daughters and sons, as individuals in their own right, the pain of the encounters they described was self-evident. This pain was caused by society's inability to accept their special children as part of the human race, and in so doing, society was 'blaming' the parents and denying their children their rights, preferring to pretend they did not exist.

Dorit Braun (1988) suggests inservice activities for teachers wishing to develop their child protection work, and these include some for confronting emotions. To begin with, these are general, exploring our own ability to discuss certain issues, such as death, homosexuality, and so on. Later, groups are asked to use a given case study and imagine they are the teacher to whom the child has disclosed. Participants then reflect on their own feelings about what they have 'heard'. Braun is careful to give clear guidelines about the circumstances necessary for using certain materials in her practical guide, e.g. she stresses the need for 'an atmosphere of trust and support' to have been established before a simulation activity called 'Cathy's story' is tried, and she further emphasizes the importance of the debriefing session at the end – since the 'exercise may prompt participants to disclose instances of abuse' and 'You should make sure that you are available during and at the end of a session to offer support if it is wanted' (Braun 1988: 39).

## Who should be included in the basic training sessions and what else should training entail?

Basic training for raising awareness of the existence of abuse in our society, for gaining knowledge about the signs and symptoms of abuse, and possible ambiguities and for encouraging emotional acceptance of a child's disclosure, should be available for all who come into contact with children in school. Some may initially question why lunchtime supervisors, school secretaries and caretakers be included in a training programme, but since they may well be those to whom children may turn because they are approachable, accessible and caring people, it is only fair that they are included. One difficulty facing a headteacher who wishes to include these personnel is finance. Workers such as these cannot be expected to attend sessions outside their working hours for free.

In particular, governors – and in some schools parents – will also expect guidance as to the school's intended approaches, the local authority guidelines, and changes in procedure arising out of the 1989 Children Act, which I will detail later.

Where possible, it is extremely helpful if other professionals and representatives from voluntary agencies involved in child protection have some input into inservice work. The importance of actually knowing your local health visitor and at least one contact in a social services department can make all the difference to how one feels about collaborative work, about attending case conferences, about simply asking another person's view on events relating to a child, and giving rise to cause for concern. All who work in schools will also need to know about local authority guidelines and procedures, and know who should be consulted within the school, should they suspect abuse.

Although sexual abuse should not be allowed to block awareness of other forms of abuse, as it is sometimes in danger of doing because of recent press reactions, it is necessary not only to cover it in a general session, but also to consider it at another time, separately from physical abuse, emotional abuse and neglect, because this form of abuse needs not only extremely sensitive training sessions, it involves issues which do not arise with the other forms of abuse, such as attitudes to sexuality. *Coping with Child Sexual Abuse: A Guide for Teachers*, by Judith Milner and Eric Blyth (1988), together with Dorit Braun's (1988) practical guide and Rouf and Peake's (1991) practice papers, would form a very comprehensive inservice pack for a school wishing to undertake its own inservice programme, although these would need supplementing with guidelines on changes in legislation due to the 1989 Children Act. Informing ourselves by reading the accounts of survivors (e.g. Angelou 1984; Spring 1987; Rouf 1991) can be part of this painful but important process.

The support and advice of the LEA child protection co-ordinator should also be enlisted, since it is important to avoid the danger of misinterpretation, or insensitivity, and a lack of confidence and competence in such matters could have this result. In some cases, the co-ordinator may suggest that she or he join the group and share the training with the Named Person, or that other trainers be bought in. For opted-out schools, buying in the expertise may be the most appropriate way forward, although such training will not come cheap if it is led by those with experience and expertise, because trainers are likely to work in pairs or teams in order to offer support to each other and to the group. This collaborative style of working is a vital aspect of child protection training. By adopting these work strategies, trainers are also acting as role models for effective, supportive networking.

### Further training for teachers and nursery nurses working in classrooms

Because they work in the classroom and are with children for long periods during the day, teachers and nursery nurses will need some further elements of training. In particular, they will be in a position to observe children. Because their basic training will have included courses in child development, these early childhood professionals will have the expertise – and with time, experience – to be aware of unusual or disturbing behaviour. Working in an early years setting, they will also be likely to be in daily contact with one or both parents, and in this case they will have opportunities to observe the manifestations of the parent–child relationship. In many cases, good home–school links can act as a supportive network for parents themselves, and it is possible for nurseries and infant schools to encourage parents to link with each other. Sometimes, the recognition that one finds one's child difficult but that other parents have experienced this too may be all that is needed for the beginning of an acceptance that parents and children in all families have periods of conflict. Further, parents with unrealistic expectations of young children can be helped by other parents to see why children sometimes behave as they do.

Teachers and nursery nurses will have had many opportunities to watch children engaging in play activities, and they will have experience of what is simply young children's curiosity, and what may be behaviour resulting from witnessing, or being subjected to, abuse. They will also notice mood swings, changes in habits, clothing and feeding inadequacies. While early years teachers and nursery nurses may have been trained in observation techniques, much of this may have related to the curriculum, and the type of observation being discussed here can often begin as the result of a chance incident which alerts the adult to be extra observant and to note facts pertaining to those findings. Because sexual abuse is rarely life-threatening in the short term (in the long term it can *sometimes* lead to attempted suicide), it is better for teachers and nursery nurses to restrain themselves from too hasty an intervention, since over a longer period, in normal classroom or nursery activities (both structured and unstructured), they may in the end gather evidence which will be sufficiently rigorous to instigate an intervention. As Anne Peake (1991: 4) states:

> . . . it is important that when professionals do intervene in the lives of children and families they do so in a way which is likely to be effective. This would involve not only collecting evidence and avoiding tipping off abusers . . . but also having a clear and coordinated professional programme of action to which those who are involved are committed. It is important that the professional network has the time to plan an intervention where sexual abuse is likely to be happening to a particular child; there is nothing more dangerous than a hasty and ill-prepared intervention which in the event of failure leaves the child even more isolated and powerless.

### What kinds of incidents should be recorded once we are alerted?

Often, early childhood educators will have a 'gut' feeling about a child, something which is making them uneasy for what may, at first, seem no apparent reason. This may be the result of tiny signals we are receiving from a child, but of which we are not overtly conscious, but once the gut feeling is acknowledged, more systematic observation may tell us why we had that feeling in the first place. There could be signs or symptoms of abuse which, because they are not glaringly obvious, or because we do not 'want' to see them, we have unconsciously tried to ignore. These could be any of those listed by Mike Shire (in Braun 1988: 55 and 67–68):

### Signs of physical abuse

- unexplained injuries or burns, particularly if they are recurrent
- improbable excuses given to explain injuries
- refusal to discuss injuries
- untreated injuries
- admission of punishment which appears excessive
- bald patches
- withdrawal from physical contact
- arms and legs kept covered in hot weather
- fear of returning home
- fear of medical help
- self-destructive tendencies
- aggression towards others
- running away

### Signs of emotional abuse

- physical, mental and emotional development lags
- admission of punishment which appears excessive
- over-reaction to mistakes
- continual self-deprecation
- sudden speech disorders
- fear of new situations
- inappropriate emotional responses to painful situations
- neurotic behaviour (for example rocking, hair-twisting, thumb-sucking)
- self-mutilation
- fear of parents being contacted
- extremes of passivity or aggression
- drug/solvent abuse
- running away
- compulsive stealing, scavenging

### Signs of sexual abuse

- sudden changes in behaviour or school performance
- displays of affection in a sexual way inappropriate to age
- tendency to cling or need constant reassurance
- tendency to cry easily
- regression to younger behaviour, such as thumb-sucking, playing with discarded toys, acting like a baby
- complaints of genital itching or pain

- distrust of a familiar adult, or anxiety about being left with a relative, a babysitter or lodger
- unexplained gifts or money
- depression and withdrawal
- apparent secrecy
- wetting, day or night
- sleep disturbances or nightmares
- chronic illnesses, especially throat infections and venereal disease
- anorexia or bulimia
- unexplained pregnancy
- fear of undressing for gym
- phobias or panic attacks

*Signs of neglect*

- constant hunger
- poor personal hygiene
- constant tiredness
- poor state of clothing
- emaciation
- frequent lateness or non-attendance at school
- untreated medical problems
- destructive tendencies
- low self-esteem
- neurotic behaviour
- no social relationships
- running away
- compulsive stealing or scavenging

Naturally, it is important to recognize that some of these symptoms could indicate other causes, and from time to time any one of us may resort to one or more of the behaviours listed; for example, being afraid of some new situation may be perfectly normal, self-deprecation may be a trait many of us, particularly women, have learnt as acceptable, even expected (although perhaps gendered), behaviour. Any such lists need to be viewed with common sense, as indicators to, but not conclusive evidence of, their possible causes.

However, some signs we do need to act on include: bruising or burns which could not have been caused in the way a child describes when asked; a young child who is clearly knowledge-able about adult sexual behaviour, who presents sexually, or masturbates excessively; suspicious injuries to the genital area; a child, or a relative or friend, actually reporting the abuse. The action to be taken will depend on factors which are discussed later in this chapter.

Anne Peake (1991) suggests attention be paid to the following aspects of observation, besides ensuring observations are carried out in both structured (e.g. story sessions, news writing, PE) and unstructured activities (e.g. home corner):

- What was the context – what was the setting?
- If the home corner or the playground, how was the behaviour related to what was going on? Might there be a *pattern*, e.g. any time the child is touched by another child or certain adults?
- What is the usual practice in this context? For example, children cannot avoid touching each other because room on the story mat is limited.
- Is the activity open-ended enough to allow children to express themselves without bias or adult manipulation?
- Are we monitoring more than just the child's play and language, e.g. body language, drawings and/or writings, clothes (e.g. if torn or blood-stained), contact between home and school? And have we looked at attendance, or rather, non-attendance? Is this frequent and is there a pattern to it? Does this 'fit' with other evidence which had seemed random?
- Do any of the children have special educational needs which may mean they are both extra vulnerable to abuse because they are physically dependent, or because they are devalued, subject to discrimination and marginalized, or because they are easy to exploit and lack the ability to protest or to communicate their experiences? (Studies about the abuse of children with disabilities include Morgan 1979; Sandford 1980; Thornton 1981; and Watson 1984.)

Most of the observations and reflections suggested above are such that they could be carried out as part of everyday life in nurseries and infant schools. Only those who are specially trained should be engaged in setting up situations intended to evince a disclosure, and even then there are those who argue against such methods, because they believe it is already assumed that abuse has taken place. Additionally, as Jan Thurgood (1990) points out, repeated manipulation of a child, or of circumstances, may in itself be abusive. The best solution is a caring, consistent relationship, in a context in which all children can be confident they will be heard and taken seriously, when they speak.

## After observing, what about the records?

Keeping careful records of one's observations is essential. It is also a grave responsibility. Records which may finally have to be used as evidence in court, or at a case conference, need to be factual, accurate, clear and as detailed as possible. First, the date, time and place of the observation should be recorded. The context, as discussed above, including any antecedents (i.e. events which may have led up to, or acted as a catalyst for, the observed behaviour), should also be noted. To this should be added the evidential points of the observation, including sketches of the child showing the position and extent of injuries, when appropriate.

The reasons why such records are a grave undertaking are that they may be vital, even decisive, in preventing further abuse to that child and to other children; but they must also be viewed from the position of the person or persons suspected of being the perpetrator(s). Teachers are permitted to keep such records and not share them with parents during the initial period of investigation. This fact has very serious implications relating to confidentiality, such as how will the teacher ensure that the records are confidential? Will the child be referred to by a pseudonym in the records, for fear of the loss or theft of such records? What will happen to the records if the suspicion appears unfounded? Will the records be destroyed immediately, or will they be kept for a period of time, and if so how long? Who will ultimately have access to such records? What if a child changes school during a period of observation, and we have not yet decided to refer the case on to the social services or the NSPCC, whichever is our LEA procedure?

It is because these issues are so important, because schools are being required to balance the right of a child to live free from abuse against the rights of an adult to civil liberties, such as knowing when a case is being built up against them, perhaps quite unjustly, that they must be discussed and attempts at resolving them made. Some local authorities may decide to issue guidelines; others may feel that schools should be left to decide for themselves. Furthermore, these questions add weight to the child-centred arguments for multi-professional liaison, or networking, since it should be possible for teachers to confer with colleagues from other professions about their anxieties even during the early stages. This can be done without naming a child or family, simply with the aim of assessing this particular set of circumstances from a variety of viewpoints, and from different professional perspectives.

The Children Act 1989 (Bridge *et al.* 1990) not only requires closer collaboration between voluntary and statutory agencies, there is also the requirement to offer support to parents and families in carrying out their 'parental responsibilities', and to refrain from intervention unless this is considered inevitable. This fundamental change in the way the law defines the relationship between parent and child, where before 'parental rights' enshrined an understanding of the child as the property of the parent, may seem to put the child at the centre of concern. Yet some critics have argued that the Act should have included provisions for removing a suspected abuser from the child's home, and that the Act has not gone far enough even though it has been acclaimed a 'Children's Charter'. Some even suggest it is an 'abuser's charter' because intervention is discouraged, and in cases where a legal intervention is deemed necessary, the time social workers and others involved have in which to assess a case of suspected abuse has been reduced. This means that the initial stages of observation and recording become even more critical in respect of the child's rights – so will workers be thought to be guilty of collusion before suspicions are declared to parents?

In order to assess whether this legislation produces the intended outcomes of greater accountability of social workers, collaboration between workers and families, and above all the child's interests being paramount, there will need to be evaluations of parents', workers' and children's views of the effects of the Children Act 1989.

### Ensuring continuity in a listening school policy

For schools which pride themselves on working closely in the multi-professional sense, and in involving parents, changes of contacts, through staff moving on to other posts, can add to the time needed to maintain these liaisons. Additionally, most schools are affected by changes in internal staffing which could result in practices related to a long-established policy being overlooked. For this reason, all school policies need to be reviewed regularly to ensure all staff, from headteacher to new entrant to the profession, are as clear about child protection in this school, in this authority, as they are about the language policy, or teaching of music and mathematics, or the home–school liaison policy. In other words, all areas of training must ensure a 'roll-on' effect.

The panel of inquiry into the death of Jasmine Beckford found that local authority guidelines at her school were shut away in the headteacher's desk, and no-one else on the staff knew anything about them (Brent Panel of Inquiry 1985).

# ELEVEN

# WHAT HAPPENS NEXT?

Because we bring to our work with young children both our personal and professional experience, some aspects of the next stages can be hard for early childhood educators to cope with, but this depends on other factors and how much say we have in how our role is perceived by our superiors and by other professionals, i.e. those working in the 'crisis' services, such as social workers and the police.

If we fear that children will be taken from those with whom they are familiar – their families, friends, teachers and peers – and that they will find themselves surrounded by strangers, then we may feel reticent about referring a case on, unless it is a matter of life and death. Many of us now in positions of authority were trained at the time when John Bowlby's (1953) work was being endorsed by government propaganda about the damage maternal deprivation would do to young children. We have internalized the importance of the family of birth and the familial home to children. Although we might now be expected to reassess our beliefs in the light of more recent findings, these beliefs still underpin the way our society works, as witnessed by the Children Act 1989, and statements by some politicians about the family, women's employment and childcare (e.g. Kenneth Clarke on BBC Television, February 1991). Even if we have kept up to date with the research on the effects of daycare, for example, and recognize that it is the quality of provision and the links with the family which matter, this research still confirms our belief that young children need continuity, sensitivity and responsiveness in their experiences. Social workers, according to the Department of Health (1991a: 5), are likely to have 'a healthy respect for parental rights' and it would seem highly likely that teachers would do also. Thus, teachers are uncertain of passing children over to other professionals, especially when all we know about these people is that they are either members of the police force or social workers who (a) do not know and are not known by our pupils and (b) have not necessarily reassured us that they know how young children 'tick'.

We may also feel that we know parents so well – perhaps mothers in particular – that we would prefer to assume that an injury which does not immediately indicate non-accidental injury, together with no other evidence for suspicion of child abuse, demands that we discuss our concerns with that parent, just as we would any other illness or injury. For example, if a child complains of soreness around the area of the vagina, or on passing urine, we do not immediately leap to the conclusion that the child has been sexually abused. Simply because the genitals are involved, why should we? If the child complained of a hurt finger, we would normally ask the child how the injury occurred and, if necessary, suggest to the parents that they take their daughter for treatment, either immediately, if sufficiently severe, or when they collect the child at the end of the day. The same process can be followed even where the genitals are concerned, unless there is other evidence to alert us to the possibility of abuse.

In a local authority which has recognized these fears and their possible consequences, a number of measures will have been taken to debunk these feelings of guilt about handing children over. Teachers and other workers will have been given time and opportunities to get to know one another, to learn about the processes, to understand the roles and approaches of their colleagues, when an investigation is deemed necessary. Additionally, a strategy will have been worked out whereby an individual child's teacher can accompany them if, for example, the mother and father are to be excluded from, or are unavailable for, an initial interview session.

First, there will be discussion of the evidence among school personnel. This will involve the person reporting the suspected abuse, the class teacher, the Named Person (senior member of staff responsible for liaison on child protection) and the headteacher. Once a decision has been taken to report the suspicion of child abuse, i.e. to make a *referral* – depending on the local authority guidelines this referral will be made either to the local social services or to the NSPCC – the matter may also be referred to the education welfare officer (EWO). There has been some concern about those local authorities which have referred cases on to their EWOs, because there have been instances where such personnel have acted as filters (DoH, 1991a) and have been uncertain of their role. The latter is certainly true in respect of children under statutory school age, since in many areas EWOs have enormous workloads and have little time to follow up cases involving children for whom they have no statutory responsibility. The Department of Health (1991a) recommends that schools refer directly to local social services departments, or the NSPCC, whichever is the recognized agency in that LEA. There will be instructions about how to refer cases on in the *Local Authority Guidelines on Child Protection.*

When a case is referred on, usually by telephone, it is important to ask the name of the person to whom the report is being made. Hopefully, if the process of personal contact making, mentioned earlier, has been undertaken, then the Named Person will be speaking to a co-worker whom they know and trust. Some teachers have become concerned because they have later discovered that their telephone conversations have been recorded, and while in a worried state they have made statements which they would not have made had they known this was taking place. This means that referral statements must be 'tight', and lean heavily on the objective records which have been kept, and that any subjective judgements, or opinions, must be separated out from the facts. As the Department of Health (1991a: 74) report states: 'how the initial referral or complaint is received and understood is critical to the protection process'. Although this report encourages flexibility in viewing the stages in an investigation, it does emphasize the importance of a planning stage immediately after referral. This may be an initial, small case conference to decide who will undertake what role in the investigation, should one be decided upon at this stage, together with a definition of the purpose of the investigation/intervention. Normally, the 'child protection process is formulated as an investigation leading to an assessment leading to planned treatment' (DoH 1991c: 82). The danger here is that a case conference may be clear about the information required, but fail to identify the worker who will be asked to supply that information. For example, in the Doreen Aston inquiry, a decision was made that the social worker require that Doreen be taken to the clinic, but no-one informed the health professionals that a report would be expected of them for the next review of the case (Lambeth and Lewisham Area Review Committee 1989).

Following the initial case conference, the production of a plan will enable the identification of causes for concern; expectations about gaining access to the home and the child for an assessment; the roles of all the professionals involved; and a statement about contingency plans. Minutes should be kept of all case conferences, including the initial one, so that future evaluations of progress can be made. Unfortunately, past cases have led to a recognition that case conferences can become ends in themselves (Islington Area Child Protection Committee 1989), apparently absolving certain workers from any further action.

The social worker in charge of the case will have the responsibility for keeping parents informed of any requirements, of process and progress, and hopefully of the expectations workers will have of them.

## Parental access to information

Parental access to information can be particularly worrying to a school. Although the best policy may be one of openness, the staff of a school may feel very sensitive about parents knowing they made the initial referral, because they may fear that other parents, as well as the family concerned, will become wary of the school. Years of home–school relationship building could be destroyed overnight if a case is handled insensitively, especially where parents are finally exonerated. Additionally, headteachers may become very reluctant to have the school named in a referral, following the action of parents acquitted after the Cleveland affair, who sued for damages. Schools will not run the risk of expensive libel cases. As a result, the best interests of one child may be overridden by the best interests of the whole school, thus causing concern for the protection of individual children.

There have been cases where schools have given totally inadequate reports to other services, because they were ignorant of the way in which their evidence would be treated, or whether the evidence would be treated confidentially between the two services (e.g. Bradford Area Review Committee 1981; Butler-Sloss 1988). If parents are to have access to every detail, if parents are to attend case conferences and hear what teachers have to say, how can reports be made as full as possible? (See Atherton 1989.)

Although child protection work must not wait until schools have established strong home–school liaison policies, those schools where such policies are already strong and actively pursued will be likely to be the ones where openness can succeed. Parents who have been supported by the school, who see the school as sympathetic to their family needs, and who know the school has their child's best interests at heart, will know about the child protection policy, and will probably have been invited to join in discussions about the school's child protection work. As far as evidence goes, there is no reason why, if the evidence a teacher gives really does separate out fact and opinion, the facts cannot be divulged to the parents; and if the school sees itself as an advocate for children's rights, parents will know that teachers will take this line, while trying to balance their interest in support of the family. There are bound to be cases where teachers feel they cannot operate in this way, that to do so risks the loss of good home–school links, and such anxieties need to be fully understood by other agencies, and if possible acted upon. If teachers do not present this type of issue to their colleagues from other professions, how can they understand what the implications for schools might be? These matters need to be discussed with social workers and police officers in multi-professional training.

## New legal orders relating to child protection

Local authorities have the duty to investigate and institute care proceedings, if necessary. The Children Act 1989 replaces the duties laid down in the Children and Young Persons Act 1969, Section 2. Also, under Section 28, the previous legislation allowed a child to be removed under a 'place of safety order'. A magistrate could be asked to make such an order without evidence that the child was at immediate risk. The child could be taken into care for a period of up to 28 days, with no right of appeal or challenge. Furthermore, the earlier legislation had been criticized because of a lack of clarity about the powers and duties of the person who obtained the place of safety order. The Children Act 1989 aims at a better balance between the protection of children at risk and the rights of the other people involved. There is now a need to satisfy certain conditions and, where an order is granted, it is of reduced duration.

Organizations such as the NSPCC and BASW put forward the argument that a place of safety order made it impossible to assess the situation in which the abuse was thought to be occurring. As a result, the Children Act 1989 includes Child Assessment Orders and Emergency Protection Orders. Grounds for the latter 'address more clearly the purpose of having power to remove the child' (DoH 1991a: 44). In the old 'place of safety order', the grounds for removing a child were less clearly defined and this permitted their use in situations which were not strictly emergencies. One of the aims of the new orders is to enable workers to gain access to children where serious concern has been exacerbated by families frustrating attempts to see children. Police powers to search and enter, and to 'detain' children, have also been altered to fit in with these new orders. Both types of order are intended for use only as a last resort when significant harm is suspected, but voluntary arrangements between workers and families, for the child to be medically examined or a situation assessed, have been thwarted. Under the new law, the duration of the orders is limited, since brevity in any legal action is thought to fulfil the Children Act 1989 requirement that the child's interests be paramount.

### Child Assessment Orders

This order is completely new to UK law. It is to be applied for in cases where a child is not thought to be at immediate risk, but where significant harm is suspected and those with parental responsibility for the child have refused to cooperate. The Child Assessment Order (CAO) is intended to allow the local authority, or those to whom this authority has been devolved, to gather enough information about the child's health, development and experiences to decide what further action, if any, is necessary. This order should not, of course, be used in cases where the other orders, which are more interventionist (detailed later), are more appropriate. Even when the representative of the local authority applies for an assessment order, the court may decide that the evidence of the child's circumstances is sufficiently worrying for the order to be changed to an Emergency Protection Order (EPO).

Only the local authority or 'authorized person' may apply for a

CAO. Three conditions are laid down in the Act, which the court must deem to have been satisfied, before granting the order. These are:

a) the applicant has reasonable cause to suspect that the child is suffering, or is likely to suffer, significant harm;
b) an assessment of the state of the child's health or development, or of the way in which he has been treated, is required to enable the applicant to determine whether or not the child is suffering, or is likely to suffer, significant harm;
c) it is unlikely that such an assessment will be made, or be satisfactory, in the absence of an order under this section. (Children Act 1989, Part V, 43)

As stated above, this order is intended to be applied in cases where the child is not thought to be at immediate and serious risk. It may be applied, for example, where parents have refused to cooperate and where failure to thrive may be an indication of some form of abuse occurring. The harm may even be thought to be of a long-term nature, but the evidence may not be thought to validate emergency action at this point. What must always be borne in mind, however, is the possibility that an application for an order may push the suspected abuser over the brink, and that in some circumstances the need for urgent, forensic evidence may make this assessment order ineffectual. The skill required of social workers in making judgements about the likelihood of immediate serious harm, of the child's emotional state and any changes in the child's physical well-being asks a lot of them, and for this reason the support of other workers, including teachers and other nursery staff, will be essential. Additionally, the opinions of GPs and health visitors, or other health professionals, will be likely to form part of this multi-professional assessment.

The CAO is intended to help workers ascertain basic facts. Older children, if they are 'of sufficient understanding', will themselves be able to refuse to consent to an assessment, in which case they will be given the opportunity to discuss their reluctance with their guardian *ad litem*, a person assigned to advise the court as to whether the child is indeed of sufficient understanding to make such a decision.

The effect of the CAO will be two-fold. First, it means those with parental responsibility must allow access to the child to the person named in the order; secondly, it authorizes the order to be carried out, according to the terms set out in the directions in the order. These directions may include, for example: that a medical examination be carried out; who shall carry it out; whether the parents' medical representative should be present; and to whom the assessment report shall be made available on completion. CAOs do offer the opportunity for a child to be kept away from home for a short period, if it is thought that the assessment would be better carried out under these circumstances, but the child's interests must always be paramount, so this is exceptional. Overnight stays must be kept to the minimum, and only used where 24-hour surveillance is thought necessary. Sometimes, a parent may be encouraged to stay with the child in this accommodation, and the CAO must detail the contact which is to be permitted between parents and child during this part of the assessment. What is seen as very important is that such an order is not equated with a child being taken into care.

The duration of the CAO is limited to seven days, in order to cause 'the least possible disruption to the child but allowing sufficient time for an assessment to produce the information required by the professional workers and parents to formulate together plans for future action' (DoH 1991a: 51). If, as was suggested earlier, the seven-day period is too short to do more than discover that further information is required, workers are urged to lengthen the assessment period by engaging the voluntary cooperation of parents. Where this is not forthcoming, yet grounds are sufficiently satisfied to warrant a further order, interim care or supervision orders can be sought, but parents should always be told in advance, verbally and then with written confirmation, that this action will be taken and what it entails. If an assessment order had been enacted, with the child kept away from home for that assessment, and the result of this order indicated circumstances so serious that it would be inadvisable for the child to return home, an EPO can be sought.

### Emergency Protection Orders

Another group of local authority professionals involved in child protection work are the legal experts, the local authority solicitors. Social workers need their advice in those cases where they are unsure about the different implications of CAOs and EPOs. Unlike a CAO, anyone can apply for an EPO, and no appeal can be made either against the making of the order, an extension of the order, or any directions made relating to the order. Similarly, if the order, or extension, etc., is refused, there is no right of appeal. If the person making the application is not acting as an employee of the local authority (e.g. if the person is a relative or friend), they should, by law, inform the local authority of their application, so that the authority's duty is enacted.

EPOs are exactly what the name implies – orders intended to offer a child protection when a serious, life-threatening emergency seems imminent. As with applications for a CAO, the court has to be satisfied about certain conditions, and the main points concerning an EPO are as follows:

- the child is likely to suffer significant harm or cannot be seen in circumstances where the child might be suffering significant harm;
- the duration of the EPO is limited to eight days, with a possible extension of a further seven days;
- certain persons may apply to discharge the order (to be heard after 72 hours);
- the person obtaining the order has limited parental responsibility;
- the court may make directions as to contact with the child and/or medical or psychiatric examination or assessment;
- there is provision for a single justice to make an emergency protection order;
- applications may be made in the absence of other interested parties, and may, with the leave of the court, be made orally;
- the application must name the child, and where it does not, must describe him as clearly as possible. (DoH 1991c: 51–2)

As was discussed earlier, there are no provisions in the Children Act 1989 for the suspected abuser to be ordered to leave the home, rather than the child, but voluntary action is to be encouraged. Alternatively, if one of the parents is not suspected of being implicated in the abuse, that person could use other laws to require their partner to be legally instructed to leave.

Although an EPO implies very serious concern over a child's safety, and possibly non-cooperation on the part of parents, the court will also wish to know whether removal of the child can be carried out in agreement with the family. Above all, the court will wish to determine the reasons why the making of such an order will be better for the child than for no order to be made – for this principle of non-intervention is enshrined in the Children Act 1989.

### Other orders

Two further orders which early childhood educators may find it useful to know about are care and supervision orders. Under the new Act, only the local authority or an authorized person (at present only a representative of the NSPCC) may apply for such an order, and these are intended to be used only when the child's safety cannot be ensured without such action. Under the 1989 Children Act, the local authority has a duty to support families and to do its best to prevent families from breaking up, e.g. through the provision of daycare facilities. As a result, the court will only grant such an order after these paths have been explored and have failed. Evidence of such failure to meet the needs of the child will require the highest levels of inter-agency cooperation, and efforts to try to provide support for families. The 1989 Children Act demands that workers always take into account the ethnic, cultural, linguistic and religious background from which the children come, so it is important for educators to truly understand these aspects of the lives of young children and their families, in order to make unbiased assessments and to ensure continuity of experience for any children who are, sadly, removed from home because the circumstances warrant it.

When children are restored to their families, the support given to the families may be crucial in ensuring the success of that return. Jackie Trent (1989) evaluated the restoration work carried out by Barnados' and found that when workers adopted the same preparation and support techniques they would have used with new families about to receive a child, the success rate for restoration of children to their own families was very high (80 per cent). In other words, where families were not given support, as has generally been the case because of heavy workloads, families were unable to cope with their children's return. While on the one hand there are strong arguments for more funding for properly trained social and community workers, adequate standards of housing, unemployment benefit, and so on, on the other there are clearly ways in which networks of support, involving a whole range of workers and members of the community, would be of benefit to families experiencing such difficulties.

## Role of the guardian *ad litem*

When cases involving children come to court and orders are made, teachers need to know what is happening to those children. A guardian *ad litem* is appointed to represent the child's interests, and since their duties include making an independent assessment of the situation, the guardian *ad litem* will usually contact the school to gain information from the head and class teacher, the Named Person, and so on. People appointed to take on these tasks have to be particularly good at communicating with children and with all those involved with those children. They may wish to spend time in the school, too, to obtain a rounded view of each child's life.

## Case conferences

The purposes of case conferences are (1) to provide information which will assist the local authority in carrying out its duties to children and (2) to clarify the role of each agency involved. As a result of the pitfalls made evident by a number of inquiries, the Department of Health (1991a) argue that very clear minutes are needed, with intended action and recommendations spelled out, otherwise those absent may fail to grasp some of the points being made. Furthermore, large case conferences can sometimes lead to such a wide range of differing professional opinions that it becomes difficult for social services to draw any conclusions. Also, the focus of the case conference and its relationship to the initial inquiry must be made clear at the outset. For example, in the Tyra Henry case, some workers believed a conference was being held as a review of the child being in care, others that it was a case discussion about protecting the child from abuse.

As far as schools are concerned, it has often been the case that headteachers, rather than class teachers who work daily with the children under discussion, have attended case conferences. While there are strong arguments in favour of the class teacher attending, and schools have to find ways of releasing staff to effect this, it would be impossible for each class teacher to attend were a case conference considering several children from the same family, all of whom were taught in different classes. In such a case, either the headteacher or the Named Person would probably attend the case conference.

Sometimes, a headteacher will take over a class to allow the child's class teacher to attend the conference, and while this may clearly have benefits for the school and the child concerned, it only adds to the workload of the head. The heads of many small schools have regular teaching commitments, and it would therefore be difficult for them to cover for a teacher in such situations.

Arguments in favour of the headteacher attending the case conference, whether this be instead of the class teacher or in addition to the class teacher, range from the experience and status of the head, to their being more likely to know some of the other professionals involved. One headteacher told me recently that she was certain she was acting correctly by attending case conferences, since when one case eventually reached the courts, she had experienced terrible stress from which she believed it her duty to protect her staff.

Tony Cline (1989) has produced a very helpful series of checklists for making case conferences more effective, including guidelines on the following processes: preparation; initiating discussion; resolving discussions and making decisions; observing the process (e.g. Did any individual(s) dominate the discussion? Did any agency appear to have a private agenda?); what part were parents, children and guardians asked to play; and, finally, self-evaluation (what contributions did you make to the conference?).

A key worker will be chosen to be responsible for overseeing the plan the case conference wishes enacted. This key worker will usually be a social worker, but sometimes a teacher may be asked to take this role.

## Reviews

The Department of Health (1991a), in surveying reports of inquiries, noted that there have been problems with respect to the evaluation of information and the fact that such analysis could have led to reviews of cases, perhaps enabling the saving of children's lives. The survey states 'The danger is that case conference decisions, when made, are regarded as inviolable' (p. 88). And it is not only social services who are accused of adhering too rigidly to an early diagnosis of a child's condition, or of a situation. The report goes on:

> There is a need to gather information over reasonable periods of time, and not make decisions on the basis of scant observation, or single sightings. What is made clear from the inquiries, though, is that judgement made early in cases can have long term consequences if new information is not let in. (Ibid.: 89).

The report then stresses that the value of a review process is its ability to ensure that deficient implementation does not re-occur.

Other ways in which reviews are essential are in correcting 'drift', that is, where case conferences have no clear records and decisions are misinterpreted or allowed to slip. Further, in some cases, ambiguous decisions have been made, as in Tyra Henry's case, where a decision was made to accept council responsibility for Tyra, but her care was given over to Beatrice Henry, thus making an apparently contradictory arrangement (London Borough of Lambeth 1987).

### Other factors affecting schools and their role

In the present climate of cutbacks, LMS, and the pressure for schools to attend most closely to those aspects of school life relating to children's acquisition of skills and knowledge, the added burden of having a due regard to children's safety, to being a listening school can seem almost impossible. When cases of child abuse come to light, staff need to be equipped to behave professionally at the time of disclosure or discovery, and in the aftermath. Finding the time and the funding to buy in training may be difficult. Spending time working with parents and governors may also be a straw which could break the camel's back. Schools competing for pupils will not wish to be seen as anti-parent, which is how some parents may interpret a focus on child protection, unless it is handled with sensitivity, treating parents as partners in such a development.

Parents may also worry about their right of access to records, and while they do not have the right to see private records made by a teacher when abuse is suspected, teachers need to take care where records are stored, especially if they might be contravening the Data Protection Act by keeping records on computer disc. The Department of Health (1991a) survey quotes the Jasmine Beckford

Inquiry (Brent Panel of Inquiry 1985), which noted that there was no centralized system of record-keeping for information about child abuse registration or statutory orders, in schools. Furthermore, when a child changes schools and a non-accidental injury has been recorded, this information should be passed on in order to alert staff in the new school to the child's vulnerability. The Department of Health (1991c) does acknowledge that schools face a problem in passing on information if they have no proof of a non-accidental injury yet are suspicious of explanations for a number of 'accidents'. The Department of Health suggests that while there is a problem of marking a child out, with subsequent labelling being a potential anxiety, by passing on suspicions about a family, it should be possible to review the school's health records periodically to remain aware of some children's patterns of experience. If by this the Department of Health means records from school medicals, they should know better than anyone that these are now too infrequent to provide such a successful monitoring system, although of course some schools will ask that children who are regularly experiencing 'accidents' be seen by the School Medical Officer, or School Nurse, whenever possible. Additionally, schools may wish to keep an accident book in which injuries are recorded if they come to light in school, whether they have occurred there or not. In this way, if injuries are accepted as being due to accidents, the patterns of injuries sustained by particular children will be able to be reviewed over time, and maybe their causes dealt with.

One major concern at the present time is the effects cutbacks are having on local authorities and their ability to maintain the necessary levels of training, including training for child protection. The employment of advisory teachers as co-ordinators within LEAs has furthered child protection work in many areas. We are far from the point where all teachers enter the profession fully cognizant of their duties in relation to this issue, nor is our present teacher workforce sufficiently trained. Many schools are still working at home–school liaison, and are not yet in a sufficiently confident position to feel they can cope with supporting parents as well as identifying children at risk. Without wishing to cause undue levels of anxiety by stressing the importance of this work, it is only by confronting our own training needs and our own lack of knowledge and doing something about them that we can begin to address the anxiety.

## Supporting survivors

Many teachers who become involved in child protection work soon become concerned about how they can offer appropriate support to a child who has been a victim of abuse. They are usually particularly concerned during the investigation process, wishing to provide a familiar and trusted adult face. Celia Doyle (1987) argues that children do need a known, friendly figure at this time, since parents may become upset or angry, the child may have to undergo a medical examination, and many other aspects of the events can be very distressing and indeed, frightening. Doyle points out that in talking to children to keep them informed, it is vital not to 'give false hopes or wrong impressions' (Ibid.: 221). For example, she suggests that children should not be told they are staying overnight with a foster family if there is no guarantee that it will be for one night only.

It is most important that teachers give children who have been abused affection and positive encouragement. Children who have suffered abuse usually have low self-esteem, and so it is essential that teachers find ways of building this up, of reflecting back to the children that they do matter and are cared about.

# TWELVE

# PROACTIVE WORK IN SCHOOLS

The complexity of an issue like child abuse and the way in which the values held by different groups in society influence their interpretation of what needs to be done to eradicate abuse mean that an abuse-free society may be a Utopian dream, but one we must strive for. What part can teachers play, besides that offering understanding, friendship and support to children, and acting in partnership with parents in the difficult task of bringing up families?

Some of the key factors identified by Mortimore *et al.* (1988) in effective junior schools include a friendly and supportive environment and a headteacher who leads, asserts their views, yet shares decision-making and management responsibilities with other staff. Both this study and that of Tizard *et al.* (1988) in infant schools, emphasize the influence good schools have on pupils, irrespective of their home backgrounds. In other words, schools can and do make a difference to children's lives, and those who come from disadvantaged homes need not be doomed to failure, even though their middle-class peers have it much easier.

If this is the case as regards children's academic achievements, can schools influence whether children are able to prevent themselves and others from being abused now, and of not becoming abusing adults in the future? Unfortunately, the simple answer is that we do not know. There may be factors which we can isolate with respect to abusive situations and we can attempt to put into practice ways of helping children to be assertive, to be gentle and to avoid misusing power, but until there are adequate data, we will be unable to tell whether or not these strategies are working. On the whole, schools which adopt such strategies do so in the hope of effecting change, but it has to be acknowledged that schools alone cannot change society.

Some school programmes in the USA aimed in particular at preventing sexual abuse, have been criticized by some for oversimplifying the problem itself, while at the same time frightening and mystifying children (Maher 1987; Trudell and Whatley 1988; Burton 1989). Carolyn Okell-Jones of the Tavistock Clinic goes so far as to state that:

> . . . some are injecting such fear and hysteria into adults, parents and children that I worry about destroying kids' basic trust and also their future mental health. Compounding this dilemma in the States is an ever-increasing commercialism and investment in child abuse prevention which is virtually creating a new growth industry, and which I very much hope we will avoid in this country. (in Maher 1987: 269)

This message is reiterated by Webster, who argues that child sexual abuse protection programmes:

> . . . ignore aspects of children's cognitive development, the same programme being presented to children aged 5–9 years as that for 9–13 year olds, and further that the programmes avoid sexuality education which might prevent a distorted, perverted, secretive and negative view of sexuality which has bred the child molesters of today. (Webster 1991: 162)

What is emphasized by both Okell-Jones and Michelle Elliott, author of a number of publications on prevention work (e.g. *Keeping Safe*, 1988), is that (1) programmes should not confuse and frighten children, (2) each professional should choose how he or she is involved and (3) no work should be started until parents, teachers, EWOs, educational psychologists, school nurses and doctors, health visitors and social workers have been consulted, and kept informed and involved. Although both Okell-Jones and Elliott have attempted to help teachers by producing and evaluating the pack 'Kids can say no', which includes a video, they argue that nothing can replace the need to ensure children opportunities for dialogue.

## Using special programmes in nursery and infant schools

Staff in one family centre (Chandler *et al.* 1989) used Michelle Elliott's (1988) *Kidscape* pack for nurseries to good effect, according to their report, perhaps because they adapted it to their own context and children's needs. The *Kidscape* programme is concerned with personal safety rather than focusing on sexual abuse, and this broader emphasis, basing work on the factual experiences of the children themselves, and intended to engender discussion, can be incorporated into the everyday curriculum of the school.

What the pack helped the staff at this centre to achieve was the development of the nursery curriculum concerned with children's independence, confidence and self-esteem, and their cooperative skills. The pack was used as a basis for very careful planning, with staff involving a consultant in their own preliminary staff training. What the consultant made the staff aware of, above all else, was their own need for time, to allow their understanding of complex issues to develop. Again, as I have emphasized earlier, this team recognized the need to come to terms with their own feelings, not just about abuse, but about implementing the programme and what may be new ways of working for some team members. Through role play, staff began to have a better grasp of the way in which children see and experience the world, so that they were able to discuss what confusions exist in adult perceptions of children's thinking. The team reflect that these experiential sessions were, in retrospect, the key to the success of their curriculum development, because without these their work would ultimately have been far more superficial. In 'starting point' sessions with the children, staff used role play, taking the part of strangers, children, bullies, and so on, themselves, and encouraged the children to 'help' the victim. Following these sessions, they observed that children would incorporate these activities in their own play.

The key features of this team's curriculum development seem to be as follows: careful preliminary staff training, with time for discussion and reflection; the involvement of parents, and keeping them constantly informed; thoughtful adaptation of the programme's suggested activities; observation of children leading to fulfilment of individual needs (e.g. being aware of the needs of a younger child who asks different kinds of questions from the rest of a group). The team evaluated their work and kept useful records, so that they were able to attend to those details which had confused the children (e.g. the use of the same doll as 'stranger' in one session and as 'uncle' in another).

Very young children will often find it difficult to understand the difference between living and non-living 'creatures', especially where these have been presented through the use of puppets. The personification of a doll or puppet may sometimes be altered by children themselves (e.g. in home corner play they decide who will be mummy, daddy, the baby, etc.), but they may find it difficult for someone to have two roles. A teacher who says she is 'Sarah's Mummy' (Sarah being the name of her child) may be told 'No you're not. You're Mrs Smith.' It is in role play that children begin to experiment with 'rules' about who can be or is what, and by the time they move on to infant school, most do have some understanding of this and of real and imagined personhood.

I remember one of my nursery pupils, Tracey, in her last term with us. It was Christmas and we had put on a puppet show for the children. One of the characters was a crocodile, not particularly realistic because we had made our own puppets. Although he got his comeuppance at the end, he frightened other characters and stole food. After the performance, Tracey whispered to me, 'The crocodile was only a puppet wasn't it?' I reassured her, showing her the puppet. After examining and handling it, Tracey began to walk away, but turned to say: 'I expect you had to be very careful it didn't bite you.'

### Problems with over-emphasis on children's self-protection

Expecting young children to protect themselves against the unwanted attacks or advances of a bigger child or an adult is patently unreasonable. It is like telling women that if they say 'No' to a rapist, he will stop and leave them alone. The power differential is too great, both physically and psychologically, and the result may be that the woman, or the child, having been the victims of such abuse, blame themselves, believing they must have failed in their attempt to prevent the abuse. Thus, sensitivity is needed when incorporating safety work into the curriculum, to avoid such a damaging outcome.

Additionally, such programmes assume that all teachers are trained and able to respond appropriately to children's disclosures, that children do not need to know about sex to take part in a discussion about sexual abuse, that children who are abused by someone they love will be able to betray that person, and that children of any age and ability can understand the concept of rights. Michelle Elliott (1988) states that it is impossible to tell if children who have experienced a proactive curriculum intended to prevent abuse, and who subsequently did manage to avoid a potentially abusing situation, did so because of what they were taught, or whether these children would have managed the situation anyway. She is therefore saying that evaluation of this kind does not tell us anything.

Krivacska, having studied the effects of Child Sexual Abuse Protection Programmes (CSAPP) in the USA, argues that 'some programs are able to teach some children some of the concepts related to what a particular program's author believes is necessary to help prevent sexual abuse' (quoted in Webster 1991: 153) and Kraizer (1986) has suggested that well-meaning professionals will often devise programmes which make sense to them, but which children consistently misunderstand. Meanwhile, Webster (1991) cites researchers in the USA who have challenged the lack of hard evidence of efficacy of the programmes, and he argues that in a society which does not accord children power, both the structures of society and children's own developmental stages render them powerless. These points are particularly pertinent in relation to children under the age of eight. Children of this age are especially vulnerable and, while liberationists might dispute the universal nature of this statement, within British society they are unable to fulfil their own needs, to live independent lives, and they are thus being asked to take on a responsibility which it should be in the remit of adults to fulfil. We should be asking if we are starting 'at the wrong end'.

I recall being horrified once, during a spell of supply teaching in a secondary school, when an 11-year-old in the class I was assigned to register, spoke to a senior member of staff about a theft of his games kit from his locker. The first question fired back at him was: 'Was it locked?' When the boy responded negatively, this teacher became furious, blaming the young victim, a relative newcomer to the school, for having 'allowed himself' to be robbed. Whatever kind of morality will this blaming of the victim engender? In a similar way, we need to change the climate which may be fostering abuse, rather than expect the powerless victims to prevent attack.

## Abuse by children

According to the definitions of the 1989 Children Act, young people are 'children' until they are 18 years of age. Two very recent reports, one from the National Children's Bureau (Bentovim *et al*. 1991) and the other from the National Children's Homes (1991) have produced startling evidence to suggest that around one-third of all reported sexual abuse is perpetrated by under-eighteens. This makes education regarding the prevention of abuse and the non-exploitation of younger children all the more vital. It also means that teachers need to become more aware of those within the older pupil age group who may end up resorting to this type of abusive behaviour, and to examine the reasons why they think this may be happening. The finding underlines the importance of personal and social education for all age groups.

## Where is change needed?

Although the study by Tizard *et al*. (1988) in infant schools focused on the children's attainments and the curriculum experienced, rather than the social aspects of schooling, the children themselves indicated concern over this as one of the anxiety-inducing factors of life in schools. This was particularly so in the case of white girls. There are two main areas of concern here: (1) the playground and bullying and (2) gender and racial factors which influence children's experiences. The researchers point out that 'very subtle patterns of teacher–child interactions may affect the classroom behaviour and attitude to academic work of boys and girls', and they add that the same may be true of teachers' interactions with children of ethnic minorities, particularly those of Afro-Caribbean and Asian origin (Tizard *et al*. 1988: 185).

Judith Ennew (1986) has suggested that power differentials lay open the path to exploitation of weaker by stronger members of society, and by weaker/stronger one can mean vested with power just as much as greater physical power. The implications of this for schools are that they need to evaluate their own ethos and structures to decide if change is necessary, so as to transmit in practice what they 'preach' in policies. Maher (1987: 210) lists seven cultural and attitudinal factors which he suggests 'contribute to the likelihood of abuse of children': attitudes to women; attitudes to violence; attitudes to parenthood; attitudes to relationships; ability to cope with money, or with the lack of it; the effects of unemployment; attitudes within the community. I would add to this list: attitudes towards children and concepts of childhood; beliefs about sexuality and sex education.

Schools which seek to promote learning that could prevent their pupils becoming the abusers of the future should, therefore, ensure that their equal opportunities policies really do work in practice: Are women represented in top management, or are they treated as 'second-class'? Are girls really encouraged to take up what have been traditionally seen as 'male' areas of the curriculum, and vice versa? Tizard *et al.* (1988) found that teachers detailed boys to mathematical activities for longer than girls, and so on. Similarly, are boys allowed to be boisterous, to infringe other children's spaces, get away with bullying, or are they encouraged to be caring and gentle, to show sensitivity? Do schools foster approaches to face and resolve conflict through discussion, or simply sweep it under the carpet? And this would hold as a requirement for staff, children, parents and governors, since it is no good adults telling children to do one thing and then being unable to follow the same approach themselves. As far as Maher's point about money is concerned, it seems the 'designer generation' of children currently in school do need this type of teaching more than ever, and the ability to cope with meagre resources is not helped by consumerism. Some children whose families cannot afford the latest gear apparently justify stealing what they want to possess because they believe everyone has it – and without it, one is a nobody, a member of the underclass (*Panorama*, BBC Television, 4 November 1991). Fostering understanding of life, responsibilities and relationships will also include tackling racism. Evidence of racist and/or sexist harassment means that a school has not paid attention to imbalances of power, and although the school cannot correct the whole of society, it can make sure that the children educated there develop their moral judgement in such matters, however young.

Developing the community as a supportive network, with the school at its centre, is one way in which schools can contribute to the raising of standards in all the areas Maher (1987) has listed. The school which chooses to be proactive in its child protection work must reflect on what is transmitted to and in the local community in relation to these points. If the young men in that community are racist and sexist, why? Have they been so badly treated by society as a whole that they feel threatened and so wish to aggrandize themselves by threatening others, or have they never had opportunities to learn any other way of life?

One area of school life which requires urgent attention is bullying. Randall (1991) provides evidence that bullying habits start early, so nursery and infant schools are crucial in tackling this before children become hardened bullies. School-based interventions should include prevention, even if cures are not thought to be needed in a particular school. Those schools which tend to be prone to high rates of bullying generally conform to the following characteristics: they are large and rarely have mixed-age teaching groups; the staff do not believe they can eradicate the bullying and therefore do not intervene quickly enough; the staff do not show consistent, caring behaviour themselves. Randall (1991) emphasizes the importance of the involvement of parents – the parents of both the bully and the victim in his opinion – and that schools need to deal with not only those issues raised above, but also the self-esteem of pupils, particularly those who are the bullies and those who are regularly victimized. Many bullies are found to have difficulties at home which they are finding intolerable. While they cannot be allowed to take out their feelings of frustration and aggression on others at school, they do need help.

Schools which ignore bullying may be allowing the development of future abusers: 'One of the best predictors of regular aggressive behaviour at 19 years of age is a history of such behaviour at the age of eight' (Randall 1991: 50).

## ✕ Aspects of the curriculum

The National Curriculum includes as its cross-curricular themes health education, citizenship and human rights. Personal and social education needs to focus on relationships, families, life with babies and young children, for nine out of ten of our pupils are likely to become parents. Teaching which raises issues connected with the cross-curricular themes mentioned above could lead to beneficial education for life. It is life-skills which many employers say they find lacking in secondary school leavers – so are we, in the education system, gradually deskilling children, rather than offering them opportunities to further develop initiative, independence, helpfulness, cooperation? If we are failing young people in their public life, are we also failing to help them develop the skills they will need in their private lives?

At Key Stage 1, for example, the National Curriculum Council advocates that children should:

... know about personal safety, eg. know that individuals have rights over their own bodies and that there are differences between good and bad touches; begin to develop simple skills and practices which will help maintain personal safety. (NCC 1990b: 12).

This is a clear message that schools are expected to address the issue of preventative work in relation to all forms of safety, including bullying in schools and abuse anywhere.

### What do we value in young children?

Becoming aware of the messages we transmit to children about the kind of behaviour and the kind of people we value is something all early years practitioners need to do. If we value, for example, reading ability above all else, the children soon take on board the message and the 'pecking order' (Crocker and Cheeseman 1988). When we are aware of our messages, we can attempt to control their effects, say, by commenting on kindness or generosity, so that other characteristics, within the reach of children who may never become the class's top reader, are recognized as valued too. What we have to remember is that abusers appear to come from the ranks of those with low self-esteem. Achievement and self-esteem go hand in hand too. If we develop schools which foster children's achievements across the board, they will also be schools which pay attention to every child's self-esteem, and the result may be that they help a child refrain from becoming an abuser of the future.

### Staff development and training

Teachers are being asked to cope with an ever growing range of work in schools, much of it demanding and complex. Training is therefore essential. More and more research (e.g. Alexander 1988; Bennett and Carré 1991) is indicating that 'teachers cannot teach well what they do not know' – we are most expert in teaching that in which we are expert. If teachers are to effect the learning of appropriate styles of conduct towards others and the prevention of future abuse, they need training. Most feel genuinely lacking in expertise in this area, despite the fact that they probably have a great deal of knowledge and expertise in: child development (needed as a basis for understanding a child's point of view, potential mis-understandings, etc.); how children learn (needed to present appropriate learning opportunities); observation techniques (needed to be able to individualize learning and to evaluate the effect of curriculum development); team teaching (needed so that children have different people, with different personalities, to refer to, different roles and talents to draw upon). It is in the areas of expertise concerned with the emotions, abuses of power and sexuality that training has often been lacking.

A further area of training which needs care is that relating to racial stereotyping. Shama Ahmed (1986: 140) points out the pitfalls of 'relying too heavily on cultural explanations . . . it is important to understand and acknowledge the cultural dimension. This awareness is important but it is not enough.' Ahmed suggests that we need to move to an analysis of the danger of relying too heavily on such explanations; in other words, abusing other cultures by suggesting that ill-treatment of a child would be acceptable in that culture. Ahmed goes on to describe a case of incest in which a social worker wrote in a report, 'This man should be told that this form of behaviour is unacceptable in our society' (quoted in Ahmed 1986: 140). Incest is not acceptable in Asian society either – and note the use of the 'our'. Training should take account of the need for an anti-racist underpinning and, as Marlene Bogle points out, there are women in the community 'who have the experience and expertise to make a valuable contribution to policy and practice within statutory organisations . . . Black women survivors have the experience of racism as a factor in the meaning for them' (Bogle 1988: 134).

Teachers of young children are encouraged to base their practice on research information about child development and how children learn. Put simply, they foster new learning by helping children 'make sense' of experiences. So are teachers, especially in their initial courses, being educated about how children may be making sense of, or attempting to attach a meaning to, their experiences of abuse?

My survey of early years courses at 40 initial teacher training institutions indicates that at least the 55 per cent from whom a response was elicited do include some training in child protection. Tutors report that students express anxiety at the thought of dealing with disclosures, and the responsibility this places on them. It is important, therefore, that they receive reassurances that they should not be left to cope alone. (This should also be the case for students on teaching practice.) When final-year students are offered posts in schools, they need to be urged to check that their induction programme includes child protection.

The possibility that such training will explore the meanings children may derive to explain their experiences may depend on the allocation of time within courses. Some concern has been expressed in the past (Torkington 1987) that initial training courses contain little or no exploration of the pastoral role of the teacher, and although early years teachers claim that they care for and about their pupils, Margaret Roberts (1986) exposed the lack of attention to children's emotional development in practice.

It is not good enough to simply assume that early childhood educators can cope because they are used to working with children at an age when they are still relatively unaffected by the niceties of polite society. The fact that one does not bat an eyelid at a child calling for someone to 'Come and wipe my bottom, please' does not mean that one is also capable of listening to and talking with children about topics like death, hate, war or abuse of any kind. Because we wipe bottoms, as well as provide for children's cognitive development, we are perceived to be very close in our role to that of parents, yet we are in fact in a very different position to parents, in that we are accountable to those parents for the way we work with their children. We do not work in a vacuum, and in some cases parents may be disturbed at the thought of their children receiving any kind of education in these matters, however appropriate for the age group. If we really value our children, then we should value those who work with them enough to ensure they are properly trained in dealing with all the facets of sensitive issues.

An additional aspect which must be acknowledged in this work is burn-out and stress. The inquiry into the death of Kimberley Carlile (London Borough of Greenwich 1987) demonstrated that systems without built-in support for the caring professionals themselves resulted in an intolerable burden on individuals. Without trust, there can be a resort to blaming other professionals, individuals and groups. Learning to live with uncertainty is especially difficult, and we need trusted co-workers with whom to share our anxieties and fears.

# THIRTEEN

# LIVING WITH UNCERTAINTY: TEACHERS THINKING AND TALKING

It was originally intended that this chapter should provide readers with some case studies about children who had been subjected to different forms of abuse, together with some discussion of the ways in which teachers, or other staff in their schools and nurseries, had worked to protect the children from further suffering. However, I came to the conclusion that one can find case studies about child abuse, detection and follow-up work elsewhere (e.g. Wattam *et al.* 1989; Doyle 1990; Richardson and Bacon 1991) and that, in any case, such disclosures to me, even if the children's names were changed, might feel like a betrayal.

Many practising teachers shared their thoughts with me. I wanted to ensure that all the teachers I talked with did not feel used, but that they felt they were part of the research process, that they had power over what ends up as the 'message' readers get from hearing about their experiences. While some have provided incidental thoughts and ideas, a small group agreed to discuss their experiences more fully, and individually. It therefore seemed most appropriate that my time with this group should explore what they, as experienced teachers in the field of early childhood education, believe are the key issues for colleagues embarking on, or already involved in, the development of the teacher's role in child protection. All hold senior positions in early childhood education, and are members of a group brought together by their local authority to provide a network of trainers, a network of expertise.

The interviews were semi-structured and very open. Carrie Herbert (1991) has raised the issue of the research methods most suitable for such sensitive discussions and revelations as those concerned with abuse, especially sexual abuse. Despite the freedom offered in the interviews, all the teachers focused on similar issues, and had very similar concerns.

## The role of the school

### Joanne

It's actually difficult for us to think of the child in isolation, I mean, we have relationships with families in early years, and we always try to be very open with parents, so we wouldn't like to involve other workers, say the police or social workers, without parents' knowledge. We work to support parents, so confidentiality becomes a problem – everyone has to be honest, I think, we can't go behind people's backs. I suppose there might come a time when I'd have to think about taking that kind of action, but it would be very rare. We like to think parents can come here and feel supported. We do a lot of home visits, outreach work. I don't know how schools which don't do that can offer the same kind of support.

### Rachel

I believe that child protection should automatically be part of the role of the school. Teachers may be feeling overloaded with the implementation of the National Curriculum . . . maybe some people think that if it doesn't apply to their particular class, they can manage without it. Schools are such difficult institutions in which to try to initiate change, too, partly because everyone's so busy I think, and after all, the main job is teaching.

It's about the hidden curriculum really, relationships in school, it ought to be part of whole-school policy to be effective in this, but people under pressure don't always see how everything fits together, can't always take a longer view, so they make lots of separate, different policies, or ignore some things because they think they can't cope with anything else. On top of that, with class sizes so big, are individual teachers always going to notice a child who says something? We always have missed children, and I'm afraid we'll carry on doing that, even trying our best.

### *Frances*

Child protection is part of our PSE programme, keeping safe, that kind of thing. The most important aspect, it runs through everything, is self-esteem, and helping children to learn how to cope, how to deal with confrontation, or with difficult situations.

It's difficult for schools to deal with the more 'iffy' things . . . children seem so sexualized. Is it television and videos we'd never have seen in our day? When I played house I made tea, not babies. You see them humping about in the home corner and wonder where they've learnt about adult sexual behaviour. Does it mean someone's been abused? I suppose teachers in 'formal' classrooms didn't – don't, get that kind of thing. At least we have the opportunity to think about whether it's something serious – or television.

I notice that parents have become more openly testy about some things too. Such as children going into the loos together. Even though it's for quite logical reasons – no locks on the doors, so friends hold the door for each other, some parents don't like it. And of course there's been complaints if it's been something like pulling other children's knickers down, even when the children are tiny . . . as though people are confused about what's normal children's curiosity, or children's sexuality, and what's really worrying.

### Inter-agency liaison

### *Rachel*

There's so little time for teachers to build up relationships with other workers, and then it can all depend on personalities . . . whether it's the inter-agency team, or an education or school team, for example, how the Named Person in a school works with everyone else, if they can accept what other members of staff are saying, one of the lunchtime supervisors, for example.

One of the problems for schools is that there's a very real dilemma about when and if to speak – you damage your relationships with the family involved . . . maybe with the whole community even, and teachers, especially class teachers don't have the time to build up relationships with other workers, so that they don't know if they can trust, say, a social worker, to just listen, not to rush into anything before they are ready. On the other hand, I suppose social workers who don't know . . . and trust, the person on the other end of the 'phone, may feel they have to act quickly because they daren't risk leaving things. Teachers who don't know the other workers might also wonder if things will be done 'their way', you know, such as, who will information be passed on to, will a small child be given the time they need, or pressurized? The problem is getting people together. It ought to be easier in the towns, for rural areas it's really difficult getting everyone together. And sometimes families must feel as though there's an 'army' of people all trying to tell them they know what should be done, queueing up to see them. I can't see a way of getting that kind of thing sorted out, but there has to be one!

### Joanne

I think one of the problems with case conferences is that sometimes you get one or two people who dominate everything, you feel as though only their view will be taken into account. Then there've been times when a social worker's 'phoned up and asked about a child, do we have any worries – if we say no, and hear no more, we're left wondering what it was all about, are we missing something we should be seeing . . . we need better relationships between social services and headteachers.

### Frances

You get a lot from working with other professionals, for example, the NSPCC social workers are so knowledgeable, so experienced, I've been really impressed by them. There's a lot of stress on teachers when they are carrying something . . . feeling they're letting the parents down . . . you need to feel you trust the other professionals, that things won't start happening immediately. When a family gets broken up, with the involvement of the school, there's the risk that the whole community will start to see you as 'them', with power over their lives and their children's lives.

And one of the problems with inter-agency work is the upheaval that's caused when someone moves on. Social workers seem to change jobs after two years or so, so when a school is involved with a family with lots of children, over a period of time, teachers see people trying different ways they think will help, and sometimes you're thinking 'We should evolve a better system, because it's the children who are suffering' . . . I'm thinking of cases of neglect . . . we wouldn't want to see the children removed from that home, but you can't help wondering . . . emotional abuse and neglect are very difficult, frustrating really.

I think the hardest part is deciding who needs to know things. Sometimes a case can be so time-consuming, or lots of different people are coming in to school, so you have to give some sort of explanation to your chair of governors. We're lucky, our chair accepts the briefest outline, no names, etc. but imagine if you had someone who started asking all sorts of questions . . .

## Training

### *Joanne*

One type of training I think we need for headteachers especially is counselling. And sometimes we get violent and difficult parents you really think are going to hit you, you learn by experience but you never know if you're making the right decisions, you just make them, on the hoof. You try to calm them down, you think about what the children have to contend with when they get home.

In a way, training is important but it can't give you formulae because every case is different. You have the guidelines, but there are so many grey areas. You draw your experience from the group. After a course you might feel 'Is that enough?', you feel very vulnerable.

I'm concerned that training seems very *ad hoc* at present, what's necessary is ensuring new staff, when there are changes, that they get training too. The Named Persons need training . . . there just isn't enough funding . . . or time for everything.

### *Frances*

One of the most important things about training is making sure you can handle what happens if there are any unresolved feelings that come out . . . we have to be prepared for this.

### Rachel

I'm worried that we'll never meet all teachers' training needs, especially at present with so many days having been given over to National Curriculum training. And there just isn't the money to take teachers out of classrooms to train them properly in term time . . . but who's going to want to come for five days of course in their holidays? Every time we take teachers away from classrooms, children suffer. Staff cuts don't help either; this not only means less leeway for someone coming out on a course, to a case conference, or whatever, it also means less time to even think about child protection, because teachers are so busy with everything else.

## Networking

### Joanne

Being a member of the group has been a great help . . . it's created a support network.

### Frances

The group's been very useful, very interesting. We've been very lucky. The meetings have helped us to think out our own feelings and responses.

### Rachel

There's always a need to off-load to someone . . . everybody has the right to be supported, right through.

The main themes which dominated the interviews were: knowledge about abuse; concern for children and families; the teacher's role, confidentiality, and the need for training and support; and interprofessional liaison, 'personalities' and changes of staffing. Overall, there was the feeling that more time and funding were necessary prerequisites for an improved system of protecting children, and that the system needed to be underpinned by child-centred practice, making the child's interests paramount.

Using Dilemma Analysis (Winter 1982, 1989), these interviews can be seen to illustrate the themes outlined elsewhere in this book, the tensions – or dilemmas – for teachers in their role as protectors of young children. The dilemmas are:

- Children in our society are thought to prosper best in families, teachers respect parental rights and responsibilities, and believe in partnership between home and school / sometimes teachers are expected to 'police' families.
- Teachers teach subjects, i.e. the contents of the National Curriculum / teachers work with individual children, some of whom need help.
- Class sizes are too large / children require teachers to have time to treat them as individuals.
- Children today may have access to explicit information (e.g. on video) about adult sexuality / children are innocent.
- An abused child has a right to expect the best from teachers, that means demands on teacher time / the rest of the class need teachers' time.
- Teachers wish to work in partnership with parents / sometimes parents do not understand about children's natural curiosity, and they may have constructs or understandings about childhood, etc. which are different from teachers'.
- Although teachers have no official, professional Code of Conduct, they do have beliefs about confidentiality / teachers are sometimes required to share information with others, outside the school or education service.
- Schools have moved towards more collegial ways of working / teachers are unsure about whether 'colleagues' includes ancillary staff, lunchtime supervisors, etc.
- Teachers have great responsibility for children / teachers, especially early years teachers, have low status.
- Many teachers are still untrained in child protection / children who have been, or are being, abused cannot wait until teachers are fully trained.

Perhaps the hardest part of all is coming to terms with one's own humanity, living with uncertainty. As Rachel put it, 'The more you think and find out, the more you've experienced, the less you think you know', and Frances reminds us of the very difficult nature of the task with her comment: 'You have to make judgements, you do the best you can in each situation.'

# FOURTEEN

# WORKING TOGETHER
# FOR CHILDREN

Whenever a tragedy has occurred, reports of investigations of the causes have frequently cited the failure of workers from different services, whether statutory or voluntary, in collaborating, cooperating and communicating effectively. This has been true in cases where the children were thought to be the victims of abuse (as in the Cleveland Inquiry; Butler-Sloss 1988) or the perpetrators (as in the case of a teenage rapist: report in *The Guardian* 14 November 1991). Sometimes this failure is between those working in different services; sometimes it is a breakdown within one service, when communication between one branch and another occurs – for example, in education, this could be between a school and the local educational psychology service.

Why is working together so important and why is it so difficult for workers to communicate, cooperate and collaborate effectively, especially when one assumes each service is there to protect children and to enhance their well-being?

### Why work together?

First, the need to work together comes from considerations of the child's or the family's needs – for a coherent, rather than confused and disparate, context. Further, the assessments, or contributions to a case conference, from differing viewpoints, bring rigour to the evidence and therefore should produce a fairer evaluation of circumstances.

As far as the professionals themselves are concerned, one would expect that the involvement of others acts as a supportive network, acting to relieve individuals from too much responsibility. Inter-professional dialogue can provide countering views at times, which will create much-needed checks and balances in situations where adults and children could easily become stereotyped as villains and victims.

### Why is effective inter-agency work so difficult to achieve?

Stevenson (1989) points out that the idea of working together appears obvious, that the high moral ground argument 'if we only understood its importance, our concern to protect children will ensure that it happens' (p. 191) is too simplistic. She asserts that life, people and situations are complex. Mandated cooperation, the result of the failure of voluntary efforts, also fails, because there is often a lack of justification on the part of those required to implement such a policy, and a lack of necessary resources. Stevenson (1989) adds that morale among workers is a key factor in their ability to work multi-professionally. Those who have suffered cutbacks, and who feel threatened and hard-pressed, are unlikely to be sufficiently motivated, energetic and committed to throw themselves into collaborative work. Even the Audit Commission (1987) demonstrated that incentives to improve collaboration in health and community care services were not only absent for many managers, but there were signs that disincentives operated in that context.

In Chapter 5, I referred to the added stress which some workers can be subjected to when working in teams, and it is likely that this is increased when the team members come from different professional backgrounds. Stress can be induced by the feeling of letting colleagues down, which results from a lack of clarity about one's role, about others' expectations and about the effects of overload. In an interprofessional context, however, there are further factors which may add to this burden. A lack of time to develop working relationships, misunderstandings about the roles of other professionals, differences in status, differing philosophies underpinning practice, together with different management structures hardly make the path of multi-professionalism a smooth one. Steinberg (1989: 121) goes so far as to state that 'because good routine collaboration between people with different expertise and approaches is the exception rather than the rule, when things go visibly wrong they tend to do so on a grand scale'.

Research on teams and what ingredients make them effective (e.g. Handy and Aitken 1986; Morley, 1990) has largely been conducted in the industrial field, rather than the 'caring sector', but it can be usefully mined and reflected upon in both schools and multi-professional settings all the same. In particular, there has been interesting research into the different roles which are essential to an effective team (Belbin 1981):

- The *company worker* whose role is to turn plans into practical working procedures effectively.
- The *chairman* whose role is to preside, co-ordinate and facilitate, give the group a sense of direction, bring out the best in group members.
- The *shaper* whose role is to motivate and speed up change.
- The *plant* whose role is to be creative, present ideas to the group concerning strategy and other important issues.
- The *resource investigator* whose role is to make resources known and available from within and without the group, and to liaise.
- The *monitor/evaluator* whose role is critical analysis and evaluation of ideas.
- The *team worker* whose role is to smooth potential conflict in the team and to be a good listener.
- The *completer/finisher* whose role is to attend to the details of plans, ensuring nothing gets overlooked.

(One person may act in more than one of these capacities, so a team does not have to have a minimum of eight members.)

The problem, of course, is that as far as child protection work involving inter-agency collaboration is concerned, there is not the least possibility of selecting the teams according to such criteria. What one has to consider in this case, therefore, is the question of whether we are all sufficiently flexible to adapt to work in different settings and different teams. Group work in schools has been found wanting – either because it simply did not happen, or because it meant children sitting in groups but working individually (e.g. Galton *et al.* 1980) – yet, properly managed, it could provide every child with learning opportunities that enable them to take on many different roles within groups at different times (Davenport, 1991), rather than their being limited by a teacher's initial perception of their strengths. We have tended to assume our leaders are born, not made, and similarly for every other role.

Thus, for adults involved in multi-professional collaboration, training is needed which not only covers the aspects listed earlier, such as the role of the social worker, police officer, etc. but training that includes role play in preparation for case conferences, to allow the adults involved to 'try on' the membership of such a 'team'.

### Theories

In addition to the other difficulties already presented, it can be disconcerting to work with others who suddenly expose their theories about the causes of child abuse, and to find that they are at odds with one's own. The case conference is hardly the time or place to begin such a debate, yet the lack of acceptance of alternative views, or the lack of coherence, may make it impossible for those with differing views to operate together effectively. Sue Richardson and Heather Bacon (1991) discuss the way in which such conflict must be dealt with, and how it can be used creatively to move forward in the interests of children:

> Conflict makes implicit beliefs explicit and it may not be possible to assess the health of a system until this happens. At this stage it can be expedient to retreat behind agency boundaries rather than be left with ownership of a problem which cannot be solved and which threatens existing social and professional hierarchies. (Richardson and Bacon 1991: 28)

Their argument is both sensible and powerful. It is important to recognize that such debates must be held and thus time, possibly during joint training sessions, needs to be allocated for such discussions and the resolution of conflict. However, as Tony Newton, then a minister at the DHSS, stated in 1982, there is also a need to guard against the paralysis which can occur when professionals put undue emphasis on achieving consensus (speech quoted in Jones *et al.* 1987). The main point is deciding what is in the best interests of the children involved, and differences in the belief systems of professionals are unlikely to be changed overnight, for they will be grounded in past histories. When one considers that individuals from at least 42 different professions and from 10 different agencies can be involved in a case (for a very full list, see Jones *et al.* 1987: 52–3), it seems naive to expect that everyone will have the same views on child abuse, its causes, family life and childhood. Further it is politicians who provide the context in which all these professionals work, and it is therefore important for them to be engaged in the debate at some point, so that they are able to evaluate the needs of workers and to assess the effects of their own policies. The debate would also benefit from community involvement. However, Blyth and Milner (1990) argue that many members of the public do not want to be engaged in the debate about child abuse, and that they simply want those who have been delegated the task of undertaking this 'dirty work' (protecting abused children) to get on with it silently.

### Lawyers – in need of the judgement of Solomon?

Michael King (1981b) raises the issue of the role lawyers must play, if a case of child abuse comes to court. On the one hand, the lawyer will often have to work with social workers whose reports leave much, as far as legal professionals are concerned, to be desired. According to King (1981b: 119), research has shown that reports are often:

> . . . riddled with inaccuracies, omissions and second- or third-hand information . . . more often than not, it is in the lawyer's interests to work alongside the social worker . . . there is no incentive to challenge anything the social worker might say, however inaccurate or subjective it might be.

There are also some anxieties concerning the type of legal system in the UK. Whereas the French system is inquisitorial, ours is adversarial – in other words, British lawyers do their best to win cases. The collapse of one recent case, investigating alleged sexual and ritualistic abuse of children (*The Guardian* 22 November 1991), was thought to be the result of one child being unable to withstand being questioned for four days. This is an example of our adversarial system in action.

## The Children Act 1989

The requirement that agencies, whether statutory or voluntary, should collaborate in the interests of children, placing them paramount in our concerns, is laudable. What we are also asked to ensure is that the family is supported, for it is legally enshrined as *the* context in which our society prefers its children to be brought up.

For some of the professionals involved in child abuse cases, their own relationships with families, through their approaches to their work, will make their participation in referrals painful, and for some, unacceptable. Participation in what some may call a 'witch-hunt' may feel like a betrayal of the parents, despite the fact that the professional involved may recognize their main loyalty lies with the abused child. The stress induced by these feelings of sympathy for the adults concerned can be further compounded by a lack of understanding, and perhaps of tolerance, on the part of other colleagues.

Stressful situations can be exacerbated by the ways in which professionals may find themselves under-resourced and under-trained for the tasks they face. In this event, they may act according to the 'barnacle effect' described by King (1981a) – practices build up like barnacles. Although changes are introduced, practices are unaltered at rock bottom.

## Positive action

The new edition of *Working Together* (DoH 1991c) makes a number of significant recommendations, including the need for agencies to establish joint annual training programmes, involving trainers from all the relevant agencies, and under the auspices of the Area Child Protection Committee (ACPC).

Other strategies aimed at improving inter-agency collaboration include: the naming of a key worker as the co-ordinator; the use of evidence from both social and medical assessments; special training for persons who will chair case conferences; the appointment of Named Persons responsible for child protection liaison work, and for ensuring on-going training for all staff; the establishment of special teams to deal with particularly complex or controversial cases of sexual abuse (Riches 1988; Osborne 1989).

## The personal and the professional

The extent to which different agencies work well together has often been at the mercy of human frailty. Since the most important people – the people at the centre of the multi-professional endeavours – are the children, it is wrong that this should be so. Unfortunately, it is impossible to rule out human weakness, and, to counter this, there are doubtless other instances where the humans concerned gave 100 per cent. What we need to explore are the ways in which human frailty (e.g. a lack of flexibility, or an inability to get on with a representative of another agency) can be overcome by the setting up of procedures.

Payne (1982) argues that even when members of a professional group do not actually work as a group, they will often behave as if they represent that group. When organizations have to work together, they may take up any one of a number of styles of teamwork. Their relationship may be based on:

- *communication* – merely informing each other of events and action;
- *cooperation* – both groups being prepared to help and support each other;
- *co-ordination or confederation* – both groups agree to change their practice, to alter boundaries, in order to rationalize their work together;
- *federation* – using, or setting up, a body to oversee and control joint ventures, while maintaining some independence;
- *merger* – both organizations are managed by the same group.

With services having very different primary foci, such as is the case for, say, education and either the police, or even social services, some of these styles will not be possible, yet variations of them exist in the nature of the ACPCs, which, in a sense, do oversee the work of the different professional groups and their ability (or otherwise) to collaborate effectively.

Cooperation between organizations is a very complex matter, and is dependent upon the level of cooperation needed for any one task, and the extent to which each organization is drawn into the collaborative work. Effectiveness will also depend crucially upon the values, attitudes, decision-making processes, organizational integration, professional co-ordination, social position, economic strength and environmental adaptation of each group. As Payne (1982) points out, the similarity in values and the styles of management and patterns of communication (organizational integration) will influence mutual understanding. So, too, will attitudes towards professional co-ordination, because this will underpin the action and caring styles adopted. Competent and confident in their own roles and positions in society, such professionals will be enabled to work positively together. Whether this is feasible in the UK in a climate in which most of the main groups under discussion have been under attack from central government over a prolonged period is debatable.

When difficulties arise between professionals from different services, informal contacts based on mutual respect can provide the links which mean the problem will be seen as solvable. If the representative acting as 'messenger' can put forward the case of the group and, at the same time, preface remarks with 'I feel . . . and I think I am right in thinking most of my colleagues would want me to say . . .' the extent to which this person speaks for the group as a whole can be made clear. Payne (1982) goes on to suggest that teams choose their team member most able to deal in whatever way is necessary with a particular situation. As a short-term strategy, I would go along with this; as a long-term strategy, I would like to see us all develop the skills needed for any situation, and to help children learn to do this.

Two further strategies for developing cooperation are the setting up of *structures* and *interchange* (Payne 1982). To an extent, the Department of Education and Science (now the Department for Education) and the Department of Health have required schools to develop the structures for multi-professional collaboration through the naming of a teacher responsible for liaison, the demand for local authority guidelines and better delineation of responsibilities in child protection work (DoH 1991c).

In many ways, interchange – as described by Payne (1982) – joint discussions, the sharing of documentation, ideas, etc., is also dealt with by the same document, in that joint training is a recommendation. If interchange is really vital to inter-agency cooperation, then workers should use the tenets of the Children Act 1989 to bring home this point. Inter-agency training (and any other interchange) cannot be undertaken without proper resourcing.

## Commitment to children

It is generally accepted that those who work in the caring professions with children are committed to advocacy of their rights and try their best to ensure children do benefit from their efforts. The Children Act 1989 is an attempt to place children's rights at the forefront. The principles on which the Act rests include the voice of the child being heard, and effective collaboration by professionals. One cannot help but be haunted by the words Michael King (1981b: 133–4) wrote over a decade ago:

> The final decision within the existing legal framework will always lie with adults. Both common law and statutes are couched in deliberately vague and general terms to allow legal and administrative decision-making concerning children to reflect the perceptions of the decision-makers as to the best interests of children. The systems are paternalistic and protectionist . . . Unless and until children are able to gain some access to economic and political power, it is difficult to see how their situation within the legal and welfare systems is likely to change, even if the proponents of children's rights achieve their objectives.

Members of the professional groups involved in child protection tend to come from the educated middle classes. As such, even those who do not agree with King's view, must repeatedly ask themselves whether, by working together more effectively, they are indeed working in the best interests of all children, or operating as a 'club' or 'team', which maintains the status quo, ensuring the passing on of cultural capital to children in their own stratum of society, while working 'on' certain families and certain children.

# FIFTEEN

# BUILDING A MORE CARING SOCIETY

We love the children of the clan. They belong to all the people and we care for them. They are bone of our bone and flesh of our flesh. We are all father and mother to them.

Briffault, North American Indian, 1956

It would be unfair to suggest that we can be, in any way, certain about the policies and practices which will ensure an abuse-free society, either now or in the future. Although we can do our best to work towards this goal, we are constantly left with more questions. The more we learn, the more we come to recognize how much we do not know. What is crucial is the fostering of a climate in which everyone places children's interests at the centre of their concerns and then work together – parents, professionals, and volunteers and politicians (Tomlinson and Kurtz 1990).

For teachers in particular, there are questions about their own role, the roles of others as they relate to the school's responsibility, and to society in general.

### Questions concerning the role of the teacher

In the current situation, with many early years teachers hard-pressed by the demands of the National Curriculum, is it fair to expect them to bear this additional burden without extra staffing? The parental choice aspect of the Education Reform Act could have repercussions for teachers in a number of ways connected with protection from abuse. First, if schools develop practices which encourage children to be more assertive about their rights as people, their personal safety, and so on, can we be sure that our society is ready for this, that parents will continue to support such schools, considering attitudes towards children generally? Further, is there not a contradiction between the requirement that children should learn to be more assertive (or is this a misinterpretation of the Health Education guidelines?: NCC 1990b) and the suggestion that there should be a return to more time spent sitting in rows with the teacher at the blackboard?

As children get older, parents may find they are startled by their children's interest in what appear to be sexual matters. Many parents expect their children to be the innocents (or ignoramuses?) our society has painted them, and it will only be those who can themselves remember perfectly their own natural, curiosity-led explorations who are not shocked. Many parents are painfully embarrassed at raising the issue when their children are older. During the earliest years, however, they may feel more comfortable about discussing such questions and behaviour, partly because they feel closer to staff, partly because their children's adult sexuality still seems a long way off. For this reason, it might be a sensible idea to include discussions about 'normal' child sexuality in any meetings with parents concerning child protection in the curriculum. At the same time, teachers could explain the regulations regarding sex education and the teaching of controversial issues.

A further worry raised about child protection teaching is: Will it mean that the next generation becomes stifled about touching other people and being touched by them? – after all, touch is essential to animals, including human beings. Most early years practitioners have managed to retain a sensible attitude towards this issue, but in conversations with teachers it has become apparent that men in the early years and primary sector do feel particularly sensitive about the potential accusations which could be aimed at them. Precautions such as ensuring one is not alone with children in an area which cannot be overlooked seem sensible, yet if we are honest about, for example, the nursery day, there are times when one member of staff may be alone with a child or a small group of children (e.g. story time, after lunch), and in some infant classrooms this must happen quite frequently. Issues of this type need to be aired at both initial and inservice levels. In whole-school training, it may be possible to decide on a school policy which covers this for both men and women staff, whether teaching or non-teaching. The policy needs also to be relayed to any new or temporary staff who join the school, and to any volunteers who come to help in classrooms.

One of the advantages gained as a result of the implementation of the National Curriculum and assessments has been the development of observation and recording techniques, and with it a more rigorous approach to judgements about children's progress in school. Formalizing the ways in which staff share information about children is one way in which teachers are improving their professional practice. Sharing opinions about individual children, supported by evidence, provides opportunities for questioning our assumptions and techniques, but at the same time it may provide a forum for discussion about children who trouble us. It may be that we find there are certain children who are viewed in a negative way by their families – the scapegoats – and it is important for schools to pay attention to the patterns of their own behaviour with respect to these children. Is the school simply feeding back to the rest of the family the ammunition it needs to rationalize its treatment of this child? Is the school in this case being an advocate for the family ('Yes, we find him very difficult too!') rather than trying to probe more deeply into the reasons for the child's behaviour, and then to act as an advocate for the child?

Earlier in the book I discussed the ways in which groups with a different approach to childrearing can be labelled as inadequate, or even abusive. In particular, white teachers, as with other white, middle-class professionals, may feel uncertain about their right to interfere in, or to judge, a family from a different ethnic group. Enlisting the help and support of members of that community is therefore vital, as is the development of an ethos in which more young people from ethnic minorities feel positive about taking up teaching as a career, an ethos underpinned by anti-racist theory and practice.

Most importantly, teachers need to maintain a balanced, yet concerned and aware, view of child abuse and protection. The majority of our children still come from homes where they are loved and cherished. By providing models of loving and respectful relationships, we may be offering the most important ingredient in protection and prevention education.

### Questions concerning teachers and multi-professionalism

Perhaps it is because of their daily involvement with all families and children, rather than intervention in crisis situations, teachers have generally played a minor role in child abuse investigations. To an extent, this relatively low profile on the part of the teaching profession may not have been in the best interests of children, but there are those who might argue that teachers are in schools to teach, not to act as social workers. While this is true, it was argued earlier in this book that unless teachers care for and about their pupils, they are unlikely to be able to teach very much, especially to those children living in distress, and as a result most early years teachers have traditionally taken upon themselves this caring aspect of their daily lives in school. However, if teachers are to decide that what they know about children and families in general (rather than those families in which children are experiencing abuse) is useful in a multi-professional context, and that what they know about pupils who have been abused is also valuable, they need to find a more coherent voice to act as advocates for children.

This will require a greater involvement in training for both responsive and proactive work with children and for supportive work with families, and this in turn will require resources. Furthermore, teachers will need time to make room for such work in their already crowded schedules.

The 'down' side of the professional development of the role of teachers in protecting children could be that, according to Susan Creighton (1987), they will have to bear a heavier share of the responsibility. Being held accountable means that when something goes wrong, social workers are sometimes dismissed from their posts, and this could become the position for teachers too. However, it is already obvious that pressure may be put on teachers to resign when a case they brought to light is not proven in court, so teachers really are at the sharp end if they begin to take a more prominent role. These issues are just some of many that need to be discussed with colleagues from within and without the education service, but children cannot be sacrificed in order to avoid conflict. Close and warm relationships between homes and schools are the best safeguards against such events, not holding children and their families at a distance.

## Questions about society today

Although the training programmes of early years teachers usually include child development, there is a growing awareness that this should not be seen as context-free, and that teachers should be aware of their own attitudes and values and the ways in which these influence the judgements they make about children and parents.

The parent–child relationships teachers are likely to notice are those which appear to them to be idiosyncratic in a way they themselves have not noticed or experienced before. What is idiosyncratic to one person, or one cultural group, may be perfectly acceptable to another. For example, Tobin *et al.* (1989) write about the anxiety of Japanese and American preschool teachers on discovering that very young Chinese children are sometimes resident at their preschools throughout the week, only going home at weekends. The Chinese participants in their research, however, felt that this was surely preferable to children returning home each day to a tired, irritable and stressed working parent, who simply sends them to bed, or leaves them with a babysitter. Deciding what is and what is not abusive, when it is a matter of childrearing practices, rather than forms of abuse about which we may feel more certain, is not always easy.

Early years teachers are important members of the multi-professional team which provides edu-care for children under five. The Children Act 1989 makes provision for preschool education for children 'in need' and, in these circumstances, teachers can be part of the support network for families. Their work may involve them in providing part of an ongoing programme of parent 'education'. Many 'new' parents today have never held a baby until they have one of their own, and education for parenthood throughout schooling can help with this. It should not only include learning about children and their stages of development, but also learning about family relationships, the misuse of power, and the stresses and strains of being a parent and a partner. Sometimes, it is argued that such learning will be superficial, even when provided at the antenatal stage, and will only become truly relevant when the persons concerned actually become parents. Therefore, offering drop-in centres, daycare facilities, parent-and-toddler groups where the 'new' parents can see older children getting dirty, playing, exploring, being awkward, and so on, is essential in our current society, where children's lives are very different from those of their parents and grandparents. Unfortunately, the ideology that suggests that motherhood is instinctive has been with us for far too long.

## The future – what are the portents?

Negative factors that appear to be related to the incidence of child abuse, such as teenage pregnancy, poverty, unemployment, isolation from members of the extended family, reconstituted families, have increased during the last decade, and seem unlikely to abate rapidly (e.g. see Bradshaw 1990). Crimes against women, such as rape and assault, are also increasing, and seem to indicate a more misogynistic society, rather than a more feminist one, which seeks social justice and equal treatment for women. We also have now the need to consider the effects of HIV and AIDS in relation to child sexual abuse (Islington and Haringey Councils 1991).

However, on the brighter side, there are more checks and balances in many areas, for example, telephone helplines are providing not only support for children, but useful information about the task we have to face in our supposedly civilized society. The outcome of the Staffordshire 'Pindown' scandal has been an improvement in the system for ensuring the voices of children in care are heard. The scandal brought in its wake a call for children in the UK to have recourse to an ombudsperson, as children do in Norway for example, and that this person's function should extend to all children whose rights are being infringed.

The influence of the UK's membership of the European Community can be seen in other areas too; in fact, the 1989 Children Act can be seen as largely the result of a movement in Europe, since several other countries had already implemented such legislation, and others – Ireland for example – are roughly in the same position as ourselves. European human rights and the European Social Charter are indications of the way in which Britain has lagged behind many of its partners in this field. The UN Convention on Children's Rights may also have been an extraneous influence which helped to move Britain towards the Children Act 1989, although some critics would say we have not gone far enough.

Although there is growing interest in studies of the position of children in society and their treatment at the hands of adults, there remains much that we do not know about childhood, the lives of our children, the effects of the technological revolution, the effects of government policies. Similarly, although there is a growing literature based on evaluation and research into child abuse and protection, it is, in the main, based on the field of social work and psychology or psychiatry. The education sector has been left behind in this area of enquiry and we need to ask ourselves why this is so.

Most of those who enter the teaching profession with the intention of working with the very youngest children do so out of a commitment to those children, and of wanting to help them learn to the full extent of their individual potential. To that end, they are primarily teachers setting about the task of fostering learning through the most appropriate approaches for each individual child and each item being learned. To be capable of such finely tuned teaching requires a teacher to truly know each pupil, to hold the key which unlocks each child's pattern of learning, and of being. Such a teacher reflects back to each child a pride in achievement, a sense of self-worth, and this itself is accomplished through honest, caring relationships for all the children who come to us as pupils. Early years education has for a long time been a sector in which home-school partnerships have been expected to flourish, where relationships could begin in a relaxed way, despite evidence (Pugh and De'Ath 1989) to indicate that true partnership is difficult to achieve and power is rarely relinquished in practice. With the demise of lifestyles ensuring extended family networks, the role of schools and nurseries has become more crucial in supporting parents of small children. Providing opportunities for parents *and* children to form their own support networks is another aspect of this role.

Community education has provided a rich fund of experience and practical expertise, but as Joyce Watt (1989) argues, we must now work at a coherent theory of community education, in order to create a meaningful framework out of the fragmented pragmatism. For people to rescue education from central control, they must fashion real centres of learning offering children, parents, members of that community and teachers appropriate experiences. With sufficient resourcing and time, such a community might be able to take some of the uncertainty out of the lives of those children who would otherwise suffer in isolation – for they would all be 'our' children.

# BIBLIOGRAPHY

Abbott, P. (1989) Family lifestyles and structures. In W. Stainton Rogers, D. Hevey and E. Ash (eds) *Child abuse and Neglect*. London, Batsford/Milton Keynes, Open University.

Adelman, C. and Alexander, R. (1982) *The Self-evaluating Institution*. London, Methuen.

Ahmed, S. (1986) Cultural racism in work with women and girls. In S. Ahmed, J. Cheetham and J. Small (eds) *Social work with Black Children and Their Families*. London, Batsford with BAAF.

Aitken, I. (1991) Report on T. Eggar, quoted in *The Guardian*.

Alexander, R. (1988) Garden or jungle? Teacher development and informal primary education. In A. Blyth (ed.) *Informal Primary Education Today*. London, Falmer Press.

Alexander, R., Rose, J. and Woodhead, C. (1992) *Curriculum Organisation and Classroom Practice in Primary Schools: A Discussion Paper*. London, HMSO.

Anderson, D. (1988) *Full Circle? Bringing up Children in the Post-permissive Society*. London, Social Affairs Unit.

Angelou, M. (1984) *I Know Why the Caged Bird Sings*. London, Virago.

Aries, P. (1962) *Centuries of Childhood*. London, Jonathan Cape.

Armstrong, H. (ed.) (1991) *Taking Care: A Church Response to Children, Adults and Abuse*. London, National Children's Bureau.

Atherton, C. (1989) *Child Protection Procedures: A Guide for Families*. London, Family Rights Group.

Attwood, M. (1989) *Cat's Eye*. London, Bloomsbury.

Audit Commission (1987) *Making a Reality of Community Care*. London, HMSO.

Baker, A.W. and Dunn, S.P. (1985) Child sexual abuse: A study of prevalence in Great Britain, *Child Abuse and Neglect*, 9, 457–67.

Baker, B. (1988) GPs in group practice are under more stress, *Pulse*, 88(6), 1.

Bandura, A. (1973) *Aggression: A Social Learning Analysis*. Englewood Cliffs, N.J., Prentice-Hall.

Barrett, M. and McIntosh, M. (1982) *The Anti-social Family*. London, Verso/NLB.

Belbin, R.M. (1981) *Management Teams: Why they Succeed or Fail*. London, Heinemann.

Bell, S. (1988) *When Salem Came to the Borough*. London, Pan.

Bennett, N. and Carre, C. (1991) No substitute for a base of knowledge, *Times Educational Supplement*, 8 November, p. 14.

Bentovim, A., Vizard, E. and Hollows, A. (1991) *Children and Young People as Abusers: An Agenda for Action*. London, National Children's Bureau.

Berger, A.M., Knutson, J.F., Mehm, J.G. and Perkins, K.A. (1988) The self report of punitive childhood experiences of young adults and adolescents, *Child Abuse and Neglect*, 7, pp. 251–62.

Berruetta-Clement, J.R., Schweinhart, L.J., Barnett, W.S., Epstein, A. and Weikart, D.P. (1984) *Changed Lives: The Effects of the Perry Preschool Program on Youth through Age 19 Years*. Ypsilanti, Mich., High/Scope Press Monograph.

Blyth, E. and Milner, J. (1990) The process of inter-agency work. In The Violence Against Children Study Group, *Taking Child Abuse Seriously*. London, Unwin Hyman.

Bogle, M.T. (1988) Brixton Black Women's Centre: Organising on child sexual abuse, *Feminist Review*, 28, 132–4.

Boston, M. (1983) The Tavistock Workshop: An overall view. In M. Boston and R. Szur (eds) *Psychotherapy with Severely Deprived Children*. London, Routledge and Kegan Paul.

Bowlby, J. (1951) *Maternal Care and Mental Health*. Geneva, WHO.

Bowlby, J. (1953) *Child Care and the Growth of Love*. Harmondsworth, Penguin.

Bradford Area Review Committee (1981) *Inquiries into the Deaths of Christopher Pinder and Daniel Frankland*. Bradford, Bradford County Council.

Bradshaw, J. (1990) *Child Poverty and Deprivation in the UK*. London, National Children's Bureau.

Braun, D. (1988) *Responding to Child Abuse*. London, Bedford Square Press.

Brent Panel of Inquiry (1985) *A Child in Trust*. London, London Borough of Brent.

Bridge, J., Bridge, S. and Luke, S. (1990) *Blackstone's Guide to the Children Act 1989*. London, Blackstone Press.

Briffault, R. (1956) *The Mothers*. London, Allen and Unwin.

Britton, R.S. (1978) The deprived child, *The Practitioner*, 221, p. 37.

Bronfenbrenner, U. (1979) *The Ecology of Human Development*. Cambridge, Mass., Harvard University Press.

Brown, G. and Harris, T.D. (1978) *The Social Origins of Depression*. London, Tavistock.

Browne, K. and Saqi, S. (1987) Parent–child interaction in abusing families. In P. Maher (ed.) *Child Abuse*. Oxford, Basil Blackwell.

Burton, A. (1989) Child sexual abuse prevention: Problems and practices, *Educational and Child Psychology*, 6(1), 31–3.

Butler-Sloss, E. (1988) *Report of the Inquiry into Child Abuse in Cleveland in 1987*. London, HMSO.

Byron, A.V. (1987) Child abuse and the role of the teacher. Unpublished MEd thesis, Warwick University.

CACE (1967) *Children and their Primary Schools* (The Plowden Report). London, HMSO.

Caffey, J. (1946) Multiple fractures in the long bones of children suffering from chronic subdural haematoma, *American Journal of Roentgenology*, 56, 163.

Campbell, B. (1988) *Unofficial Secrets*. London, Virago.

Campbell, B. (1990) Seen but not heard, *Marxism Today*, November, pp. 20–22.

Campbell, B. and Sedley, S. (1988) A family tragedy, *Marxism Today*, July, pp. 16–19.

Campbell, R.J. and Neill, S.St.J. (1990) *Teacher Time in Key Stage 1*. London, AMMA.

Castle, R. (1976) *Case Conferences: A Cause for Concern?* London, NSPCC.

Chandler, S., Stone, R. and Young, E. (1989) Learning to say 'No', *Child Education*, 66(4), 15–17.

Clarke, A.M. and Clarke, A.D.B. (eds) (1976) *Early Experience: Myth and Evidence*. London, Gordon and Breach.

Cline, T. (1989) Making case conferences more effective, *Children and Society*, 3(2), 99–106.

Cochran, M. (1986) The parental empowerment process building on family strengths. In J. Harris (ed.) *Child Psychology in Action*. London, Croom Helm.

Coffield, F. (1983) Like father, like son. In N. Madge (ed.) *Families at Risk*. London, Faber and Faber.

Cooper, C.L. and Payne, R. (eds) (1980) *Current Concerns in Occupational Stress*. Chichester, John Wiley.

Cooper, J. (1987–8) Family affairs. In W. Stone and C. Warren (eds) *Protection or Prevention*. London, Child Care NCVCCO.

Corby, B. (1987) *Working with Child Abuse*. Milton Keynes, Open University Press.

Corby, B. (1989) Alternative theory bases in child abuse. In W. Stainton Rogers, D. Hevey and E. Ash (eds) *Child Abuse and Neglect: Facing the Challenge*. London, Batsford/Milton Keynes, Open University.

Corby, B. (1990) Making use of child protection statistics, *Children and Society*, 4(3), 304–14.

Cornwell, J. (1991) *Powers of Darkness, Powers of Light*. London, Viking.

Creighton, S. (1987) Quantitative assessment of child abuse. In P. Maher (ed.) *Child Abuse*. Oxford, Basil Blackwell.

Croale, A. (1986) Behind the panel, *Community Care*, 17 April, pp. 24–25.

Crocker, A.C. and Cheeseman, R.G. (1988) Infant teachers have a major impact on children's self-awareness, *Children and Society*, 2(1), 3–8.

Dahlberg, G. (1991) Empathy and social control. On parent–child relations in the context of modern childhood. Paper presented at the ISSBD Conference in Minneapolis, USA.

Dahlstrom, E. (1989) Theories and ideologies of family functions, gender relations and human reproduction. In K. Boh, M. Bak, C. Clason, M. Pankratova, J. Qvortup, B.G. Sgritta and K. Aerness (eds) *Changing Patterns of European Family Life*. London, Routledge.

Dale, P., Davies, M., Morrison, T. and Waters, J. (1986) *Dangerous Families*. London, Tavistock.

Davenport, C.A. (1991) The role of the individual in cooperative and collaborative group work. Unpublished M.A. thesis, Warwick University.

David, T. (1990) *Under Five – Under-educated?* Milton Keynes, Open University Press.

Dawkins, R. (1976) *The Selfish Gene*. Oxford, Oxford University Press.

De Mause, L. (ed.) (1974) *The History of Childhood*. New York, Psychohistory Press.

Department of Education and Science (1978) *Primary Education in England: A Survey by Her Majesty's Inspectors of Schools*. London, HMSO.

Department of Education and Science (1988) *Working Together for the Protection of Children from Abuse: Procedures for the Education Service*. London, HMSO.

Department of Education and Science (1989) *Discipline in Schools* (The Elton Report). London, HMSO.

Department of Education and Science (1990) Alan Howarth welcomes local authority action on child abuse, *DES News*, 254/90.

Department of Health (1988) *Protecting Children: A Guide for Social Workers Undertaking a Comprehensive Assessment*. London, HMSO.

Department of Health (1990) *An Introduction to the Children Act 1989*. London, HMSO.

Department of Health (1991a) *Child Abuse: A Study of Inquiry Reports 1980–1989*. London, HMSO.

Department of Health (1991b) *The Children Act 1989: Guidance and Regulations Vol. 1, Court Orders*. London, HMSO.

Department of Health (1991c) *Working Together*. London, HMSO.

Department of Health and Social Security (1968) *Report of the Committee on Local Authority and all the Personal Social Services*, Cmnd 3703 (The Seebohm Report). London, HMSO.

Department of Health and Social Security (1982) *Child Abuse: A Study of Inquiry Reports*. London, HMSO.

Department of Health and Social Security (1986) *Child Abuse – Working Together for the Protection of Children* (draft circular). London, DHSS.

Department of Health and Social Security (1988) *Working Together*. London, HMSO.

Donzelot, J. (1980) *Policing the Family*. London, Hutchinson.

Doyle, C. (1987) Sexual abuse: Giving help to children, *Children and Society*, 1(3), 210–23.

Doyle, C. (1990) *Working with Abused Children*. London, Macmillan/ BASW.

Driver, E. (1989) Introduction. In E. Driver and A. Droisen (eds) *Child Sexual Abuse: Feminist Perspectives*. London, Macmillan.

Droisen, A. (1989) Some biographies. In E. Driver and A. Droisen (eds) *Child Sexual Abuse: Feminist Perspectives*. London, Macmillan.

Dunn, J. (1987) Understanding feelings: The early stages. In J. Bruner and H. Haste (eds) *Making Sense*. London, Methuen.

Dyer, C. (1987) First High Court judgement on sex abuse in Cleveland, *British Medical Journal*, 8 August, 18, p. 382.

Elliott, M. (1988) *Keeping Safe*. Sevenoaks, Hodder and Stoughton.

Elliott, M. (1988 ) *Kidscape Under-Fives' Programme* (pack for nurseries). London, Kidscape.

Ennew, J. (1986) *The Sexual Exploitation of Children*. Cambridge, Polity Press.

Finkelhor, D. (1983) Common features of family abuse. In D. Finkelhor, R.J. Gelles, G.T. Hotaling and M.A. Straus (eds) *The Dark Side of Families*. London, Sage.

Finkelhor, D. (1988) The trauma of sexual abuse: Two models. In G. Wyatt and G.J. Powell (eds) *Lasting Effects of Child Sexual Abuse*. London, Sage.

Finkelhor, D. and Korbin, J.E. (1988) Child abuse as an international issue, *Child Abuse and Neglect*, 12(1), 3–23.

Finkelhor, D., Araji, S., Baron, L., Browne, A., Doyle Peters, S. and Wyatt G.E. (1986) *A Sourcebook on Child Sexual Abuse*. London, Sage.

Foster, M. (1988–9) The French Puericultrice, *Children and Society*, 2(4), 319–34.

Freeman, M. (1983) *The Rights and Wrongs of Children*. London, Francis Pinter.

Freeman, M. (1987) Child care and the law. In W. Stone and C. Warren (eds) *Protection or Prevention*. London, Child Care NCVCCO.

Freeman, M. (1988) Time to stop hitting our children, *Childright*, 51, 5.

Furniss, T.H. (1987) An integrated treatment approach to child sexual abuse within the family, *Children and Society*, 1(2), 123-35.

Galton, M., Simon, B. and Croll, P. (1980) *Inside the Primary Classroom*. London, Routledge and Kegan Paul.

Gelles, J. (1973) Child abuse as psychopathology: A sociological critique and reformulation, *American Journal of Orthopsychiatry*, 43, 611-21.

Gelles, J. and Straus, M.A. (1987) Is violence towards children increasing? *Journal of Interpersonal Violence*, 2(2), 212-22.

Germain, C. and Gitterman, A. (1980) *The Life Model of Social Work Practice*. Cambridge, Mass., Harvard University Press.

Gibbons, J., Thorpe, S. and Wilkinson, P. (1990) *Family Support and Prevention: Studies in Local Areas*. London, HMSO.

Gilmour, A. (1988) *Innocent Victims: Questions of Child Abuse*. London, Michael Joseph.

Gittins, D. (1985) *The Family in Question*. Basingstoke, Macmillan.

Glaser, D. and Frosh, S. (1988) *Child Sexual Abuse*. London, Macmillan Educational.

Goldman, R. and Goldman, J. (1982) *Children's Sexual Thinking*. London, Routledge and Kegan Paul.

Goldman, R. and Goldman, J. (1988) *Show Me Yours: What Children Think About Sex*. Harmondsworth, Penguin.

Gough, D.A. (1991) Preventive educational programmes for children. In K. Murray and D.A. Gough (eds) *Intervening in Child Sexual Abuse*. Edinburgh, Scottish Academic Press.

Griffiths, D.L. and Moynihan, F.J. (1963) Medical epiphyseal injuries in babies (Battered Baby Syndrome), *British Medical Journal*, 295, 382.

*Guardian, The* (1991) Abuse case told of care boy's 'friend', *The Guardian* 1 October.

Hall, L. and Lloyd, S. (1989) *Surviving Child Sexual Abuse*. London, Falmer Press.

Hamilton, L.R. (1989) Variables associated with child maltreatment and implications for prevention and treatment. In J.T. Pardeck (ed.) *Child Abuse and Neglect: Theory, Research and Practice*. New York, Gordon and Breach.

Handy, C. and Aitken, R. (1986) *Understanding Schools as Organisations*. Harmondsworth, Penguin.

Hazell, T. (1987) Research, ideology and practice – a discontinuity, *Children and Society*, 1(1), 51-7.

Herbert, C. (1991) Working together to protect children: An educationist's perspective. Lecture, Kellmer Pringle Award Seminar Series, Warwick University, 20 October.

Herbert, E. (1990) Disclosure of Down's Syndrome: Recollections of ten mothers. Unpublished study, BPhil (ed.) degree course, Warwick University.

Hobbs, C.J. and Wynne, J.M. (1986) Buggery in childhood – a common syndrome of child abuse, *Lancet*, 8510, 4 October, pp. 792–6.

Holman, B. (1988) *Putting Families First. Prevention and Child Care: A Study of Prevention by Voluntary and Statutory Agencies*. Basingstoke, Macmillan.

Homan, G. (1958) Social behaviour as exchange, *American Journal of Sociology*, 63, 597–606.

Hughes, M., Wikeley, T. and Nash, T. (1991) *Parents and SATs: A Second Interim Report*. Exeter, Exeter University School of Education.

Islington Area Child Protection Committee (1989) *Inquiry into the Death of Liam Johnson*. London, Islington Borough Council.

Islington and Haringey Councils (1991) *HIV/AIDS and Young Children*. London, Islington and Haringey Councils.

Jones, D.N., Pickett, J., Oates, M.R. and Barbor, P.R.H. (1987) *Understanding Child Abuse*. London, Macmillan Educational.

Kempe, C.H., Silverman, F.N., Steele, B.B., Droegemueller, W. and Silver, H.K. (1962) The battered child syndrome, *Journal of the American Medical Association*, 181, pp. 17–24.

Kempe, R.S. and Kempe, C.H. (1978) *Child Abuse*. London, Fontana.

King, M. (1981a) *Research into Residential Care: Guidance for Decision-makers*. Aberdeen, Aberdeen University Highlights.

King, M. (1981b) *Childhood, Welfare and Justice*. London, Batsford.

King, R. A. (1978) *All Things Bright and Beautiful?* Chichester, John Wiley.

Kitzinger, J. (1990) Who are you kidding? Power and the struggle against sexual abuse. In A. James and A. Prout (eds) *Constructing and Reconstructing Childhood*. London, Falmer Press.

Kohlberg, L. (1969) Stage and sequence: The cognitive developmental approach to socialization. In D. Goslin (ed.) *Handbook of Socialization Theory and Research*. Chicago, Rand-McNally.

Korbin, J.E. (1980) The cultural context of child abuse and neglect, *Child Abuse and Neglect*, 4(1), 3–13.

Korbin, J.E. (1981) Introduction: Etiology of child abuse and neglect. In *Child Abuse and Neglect: Cross-cultural Perspectives*. Berkeley, Calif., University of California Press.

Kraizer, S.K. (1986) Re-thinking prevention, *Child Abuse and Neglect*, 10, 259–61.

La Fontaine, J. (1990) *Child Sexual Abuse*. Cambridge, Polity Press.

La Fontaine, J. (1991) *Bullying: The Child's View*. London, Gulbenkian Foundation.

Lambeth and Lewisham Area Review Committee (1989) *Inquiry into the Death of Doreen Aston*. London, Lambeth and Lewisham.

Lasch, C. (1977) *Haven in a Heartless World*. New York, Basic Books.

Lefkowitz, M.M., Eron, L.D., Walder, L.O. and Huesmann, L.R. (1977) *Growing Up to be Violent*. New York, Pergamon Press.

Lewis, A. (1990) Six and seven-year-old children's talk to peers with severe learning difficulties, *European Journal of Special Needs Education*, 5(1), 13–23.

Lewis, J. (1986) Anxieties about the family. In M. Richards and P. Light (eds) *Children of Social Worlds*. Cambridge, Polity Press.

London Borough of Greenwich (1987) *Inquiry into the Death of Kimberley Carlile*. London, Greenwich Borough Council.

London Borough of Lambeth (1987) *Inquiry into the Death of Tyra Henry*. London, Lambeth Borough Council.

Lynch, M.A. and Roberts, J. (1982) *Consequences of Child Abuse*. London, Academic Press.

Lyon, C. and de Cruz, P. (1990) *Child Abuse*. Bristol, Family Law/Jordan and Co.

Maccoby, E.E. (1980) *Social Development: Psychological Growth and the Parent-Child Relationship*. New York, Harcourt Brace Jovanovich.

MacLeod, M. and Saraga, E. (1987) Abuse of power, *Marxism Today*, 8, 10–13.

MacLeod, M. and Saraga, E. (1988) Challenging the orthodoxy: Towards a feminist theory and practice, *Feminist Review*, 28, 16–55.

Maher, P. (ed.) (1987) *Child Abuse: The Educational Perspective*. Oxford, Basil Blackwell.

Manning, M., Heron, J. and Marshall, T. (1978) Styles of hostility and social interactions at nursery, at school, and at home: an extended study of children. In L.A. Hertsov and M. Berger (eds) *Aggression and Antisocial Behaviour in Childhood and Adolescence*. New York, Pergamon Press.

Martin, H.P. and Beezley, P. (1977) Behavioural observations of abused children, *Developmental Medicine and Child Neurology*, 19, 373–87.

McLean, S.V. (1991) *The Human Encounter: Teachers and Children Living Together in Pre-schools*. London, Falmer Press.

Melhuish, E. (1991) Research on daycare for young children in the United Kingdom. In E. Melhuish and P. Moss (eds) *Day Care for Young Children*. London, Routledge.

Mettlin, C. and Woelfel, J. (1974) Interpersonal influence and symptoms of stress, *Journal of Health and Social Behaviour*, 15(4), 311–19.

Miller, A. (1987) *For Your Own Good*. London, Virago.

Miller, A. (1991) *Banished Knowledge*. London, Virago.

Miller, L. (1980) Eileen, *Journal of Child Psychotherapy*, 6, 57–67.

Milner, J. and Blyth, E. (1988) *Coping with Child Sexual Abuse: A Guide for Teachers*. Harlow, Longman.

Mitchell, C. (1973) *Time for School*. Harmondsworth, Penguin.

Morgan, S.R. (1979) Psycho-educational profile of emotionally disturbed abused children, *Journal of Clinical Child Psychology*, 8(1), 3–6.

Morley, I.E. (1990) Building cross-functional design teams. In Proceedings of the First International Conference on Integrated Design Management, pp. 100–110, IFS Conferences.

Mortimore, P., Sammons, P., Stoll, L., Lewis, D. and Ecob, R. (1988) *School Matters*. Wells, Open Books.

National Children's Homes (1991) *Report of the Committee of Enquiry into Children and Young People who Abuse other Children*. London, National Children's Homes.

National Curriculum Council (1990a) *Education for Citizenship*. York, NCC.

National Curriculum Council (1990b) *Health Education*. York, NCC.

National Society for the Prevention of Cruelty to Children (1989) *Child Abuse Trends in England and Wales 1983–1987*. London, NSPCC.

National Society for the Prevention of Cruelty to Children (1991) *Child Abuse Investigations: A Guide for Children and Young People*. London, NSPCC.

National Union of Teachers (1991) *Miss, the Rabbit Ate the 'Floating' Apple: The Case Against SATs*. London, NUT.

Newell, P. (1989) *Children are People Too*. London, Bedford Square Press.

Newson, J. and Newson, E. (1963) *Infant Care in an Urban Community*. London, George Allen and Unwin.

Newson, J. and Newson, E. (1968) *Four Years Old in an Urban Community*. London, George Allen and Unwin.

Osborne, A. (1989) Interagency work in child protection. In W. Stainton Rogers, D. Hevey and E. Ash (eds) *Child Abuse and Neglect: Facing the Challenge*. London, Batsford/Milton Keynes, Open University.

Parton, N. (1985) *The Politics of Child Abuse*. London, Macmillan.

Payne, M. (1982) *Working in Teams*. London, Macmillan Educational/BASW.

Peake, A. (1989a) Child sexual assault prevention programmes in school. In K. Rouf and A. Peake, *Working with Sexually Abused Children: A Resource Pack for Professionals*. London, The Children's Society.

Peake, A. (1989b) Issues of under-reporting: The sexual abuse of boys, *Educational and Child Psychology*, 6(1), 42–50.

Peake, A. (1991) Dealing with the suspicion of child sexual abuse: the role of the class teacher. In G. Lindsay and A. Miller (eds) *Psychology Services to Primary Schools*. London, Longmans.

Pleck, E. (1987) *Domestic Tyranny*. Oxford, Oxford University Press.

Pollard, A. and Tann, S. (1987) *Reflective Teaching in the Primary School*. London, Cassell.

Postman, N. (1985) *The Disappearance of Childhood*. London, Comet/W.H. Allen.

Pringle, M.K. (1974) *The Needs of Children*. London, Hutchinson.

Pugh, G. (1987) Early education and daycare: In search of a policy, *Journal of Education Policy*, 2(4), 301–16.

Pugh, G. and De'Ath, E. (1989) *Working Towards Partnership in the Early Years*. London, National Children's Bureau.

Randall, P. (1991) Bullies and their victims, *Child Education*, 68(3), 50–1.

Rapoport, R. and Moss, P. (1990) *Men and Women as Equals at Work*. London, Thomas Coram Research Centre.

Rathbone, E. (1924) *The Disinherited Family*. London, Arnold.

Reid, K. (1989) Bullying and persistent school absenteeism. In D.P. Tattum and D.A. Lane (eds) *Bullying in Schools*. Stoke-on-Trent, Trentham Books.

Richardson, S. and Bacon, H. (1991) *Child Sexual Abuse: Whose Problem?* Birmingham, Venture Press.

Riches, P. (1988) Working together for whose benefit? *Children and Society*, 2(3), 270–8.

Roberts, M. (1986) *Educating Young Children's Emotions*. WEF Annual Conference, Kingston Polytechnic, London, May.

Roberts, S.R. (1986) Examination of the anus in suspected child sexual abuse, *Lancet*, No. 8515, 8 November, p. 1100.

Rouf, K. (1991) My self in echoes. My voice in song. In A. Bannister, K. Barrett and E. Shearer (eds) *Listening to Children*. Harlow, Longman.

Rouf, K. and Peake, A. (1991) *Working with Sexually Abused Children: A Resource Pack for Professionals*. London, The Children's Society.

Sandford, L. (1980) *The Silent Children: A Parents' Guide to the Prevention of Child Sexual Abuse*. London, Doubleday.

Schaffer, H.R. (1990) *Making Decisions about Children*. Oxford, Basil Blackwell.

Segal, L. (1989) The beast in man, *New Statesman and Society*, 118, 21–5.

Sharron, H. (1987) The influence of the Paterson factor, *Social Work Today*, 30 March, pp. 8–9.

Shemmings, D. and Thoburn, J. (1990) *Parental Participation in Child Protection Conferences*. Norwich, University of East Anglia.

Shorter, E. (1976) *The Making of the Modern Family*. New York, Basic Books.

Slukin, A. (1981) *Growing Up in the Playground*. London, Routledge and Kegan Paul.

Sommerville, J. (1982) *The Rise and Fall of Childhood*. Beverly Hills, Calif., Sage.

Spencer, J.R. and Flin, R. (1990) *The Evidence of Children: The Law and the Psychology*. London, Blackstone.

Spring, J. (1987) *Cry Hard and Swim: The Story of an Incest Survivor*. London, Virago.

Staffordshire Child Care Inquiry Team (1991) *The Pindown Experience and the Protection of Children*. Stafford, Staffordshire County Council.

Steedman, C. (1990) *Childhood, Class and Culture in Britain: Margaret McMillan*. London, Virago.

Steinberg, D. (1989) *Interprofessional Consultation*. Oxford, Basil Blackwell.

Stephenson, P. and Smith, D. (1989) Bullying in the junior school. In D.P. Tattum and D.A. Lane (eds) *Bullying in Schools*. Stoke-on-Trent, Trentham Books.

Stevenson, O. (ed.) (1989) *Child Abuse: Public Policy and Professional Practice*. London, Harvester-Wheatsheaf.

Stone, F. (ed.) (1989) *Child Abuse: The Scottish Experience*. London, BAAF.

Stone, M. (1988) *Social Work Training for Child Protection Work*. Guildford, University of Surrey Department of Educational Studies.

Straus, M., Gelles, R. and Steinmetz, K. (1980) *Behind Closed Doors: Violence in the American Family*. New York, Anchor Press.

Suransky, V.P. (1982) *The Erosion of Childhood*. Chicago, Chicago University Press.

Szur, R. (1987) Emotional abuse and neglect. In P. Maher (ed.) *Child Abuse: The Educational Perspective*. Oxford, Basil Blackwell.

Thompson, E.P. (1980) *The Making of the English Working Class*. Harmondsworth, Penguin.

Thompson, F. (1945) *Lark Rise to Candleford*. Oxford, Oxford University Press.

Thornton, V. (1981) Growing up with cerebral palsy. In D.G. Bullard and S.E. Knight (eds) *Sexuality and Physical Disability*. London, C.V. Mosby.

Thurgood, J. (1990) Active listening: A social services perspective. In A. Bannister, K. Barrett and E. Shearer (eds) *Listening to Children*. Harlow, Longman.

Tizard, B., Blatchford, P., Burke, J., Farquhar, C. and Plewis, I. (1988) *Young Children at School in the Inner City*. Hove, Lawrence Erlbaum Associates Ltd.

Tobin, J.J., Wu, D.H.A. and Davidson, D.H. (1989) *Preschool in Three Cultures*. New Haven, Conn., Yale University Press.

Tomlinson, J.R.G. and Kurtz, Z. (1990) Attitudes to children: Are children valued? RSA Inaugural Lecture.

Torkington, K. (1987) Working group two report back. In P. Maher (ed.) *Child Abuse*. Oxford, Basil Blackwell.

Trent, J. (1989) *Homeward Bound: The Rehabilitation of Children to their Birth Parents*. London, Barnado's.

Trudell, M.S. and Whatley, M.H. (1988) School sexual abuse prevention: Unintended consequences and dilemmas, *Child Abuse and Neglect*, 12, 103–13.

Tunnard, J. (1987–8) Family Rights. In W. Stone and C. Warren (eds)

*Protection or Prevention*. London, Child Care/National Council of Voluntary Child Care Organisations.

United Nations (1989) *Convention on the Rights of the Child*. London, UNICEF.

Vizard, E. (1987) The historical and cultural context of abuse. In P. Maher (ed.) *Child Abuse*. Oxford, Basil Blackwell.

Voluntary Organisations Liaison Council for Under Fives (1990) *Child Abuse: A Guide for Under Five Workers*. London, VOLCUF.

Vondra, J.I. and Toth, S.L. (1989) Child maltreatment research and intervention. In J.T. Pardeck (ed.) *Child Abuse and Neglect: Theory, Research and Practice*. New York, Gordon and Breach.

Washburne, C. (1983) A feminist analysis of child abuse and neglect. In D. Finkhelor, R. Gelles, G. Hotaling and M. Straus (eds) *The Dark Side of Families*. New York, Sage.

Watson, J.D. (1984) Talking about the best-kept secret, *The Exceptional Parent*, September, pp. 15–20.

Watt, J. (1989) Community education and parent involvement: A partnership in need of a theory. In F. Macleod (ed.) *Parents and Schools: The Contemporary Challenge*. London, Falmer Press.

Watt, J. (1990) *Early Education: The Current Debate*. Edinburgh, Scottish Academic Press.

Wattam, C. (1990) *Teachers' Experiences with Children Who Have or May Have Been Sexually Abused*. London, NSPCC.

Wattam, C., Hughes, J. and Blagg, H. (1989) *Child Sexual Abuse*. Harlow, Longman.

Webster, R. (1991) Issues in school-based child sexual abuse prevention, *Children and Society*, 5(2), 146–64.

Weissman, H., Epstein, I. and Savage, A. (1983) *Agency Based Social Work: Neglected Aspects of Clinical Practice*. Colerado, Temple University Press.

Winnicott, D.W. (1964) *The Child, the Family and the Outside World*. Harmondsworth, Penguin.

Winter, R. (1982) Dilemma analysis: A contribution to methodology for action research, *Cambridge Journal of Education*, 12(3), 161–74.

Winter, R. (ed.) (1989) *Learning from Experience*. London, Falmer Press.

# INDEX